The Amazing Tragic

The Amazing Tragic

Jeffrey Bovee

Dedicated to my family that provides me the strength to continue.

Thank you, Stephanie, Aidan, Julian, Eileen, Arlene, Lenny Jr., Jenna, Leonard Sr. and John

Foreword

I met Jeff Bovee at Anna Devine Elementary School in Rifton, NY. I think it was the fifth or sixth grade. I remember him being the new kid on the block. I don't remember welcoming him as I had my group of friends that I had built around me like a comfortable blanket. I was that smart kid – the one that waited for friends to find me instead of making friends happen.

Jeff and I followed each other through Kingston High School. We knew of each other because we both wanted to be musicians and were in the band scene. We probably jammed a few songs together at some point, but I was still the smart, geeky kid. Jeff was the cool musician kid that was growing up a lot faster than me. We all knew that Jeff wasn't taking the straight path in life, but we had no idea that we could have reached out and possibly changed where he was headed. Parts of us wanted to join him.

A few weeks ago, my wife and I watched "The Breakfast Club." If you've seen it, you realize that we have the power to change lives if we just listen to what others say and encourage those discussions to happen. We can also be hurtful and cruel without even trying. I'd like to think Jeff didn't see me as judgmental when we were in school. But I probably kept my distance and silently passed that judgement through quiet actions and I certainly didn't do anything to challenge his drug use.

After high school, my friends and I went off to college. Jeff had disappeared. I remember wondering where he went. Before email, texts and Facebook, we relied on the rumor mill for news. Jeff and I still had some mutual friends, but, within a few years, our lives had clearly separated and we lost touch completely.

Fast forward to a few years ago and Jeff pops up on my Facebook feed. I thought to myself, "Cool, he's still kicking! I wonder what he's up to?" Jeff's pics showed some kids, a beautiful girlfriend and a seemingly normal life. But then, Facebook never shows your true self.

Everyone knew something was wrong when Jeff posted a GoFundMe page for himself, but I had no idea of the magnitude of his problems. I wanted to help, but who in their right mind would fund a junkie that's using the Internet to source funds? But something pulled on me. I felt guilty about not contributing. Shortly thereafter, Jeff disappeared again.

In Jeff's world, he was now in Orange County Jail where he started writing the notes that form this book. When he was released, he posted some of the first chapters to his Facebook page. When I read his words, I felt everything. You'll have to read it yourself to understand. Knowing Jeff as a kid made his words hit close to home. They had a strength and an impact that woke something up inside of me. This story happened in my old school, to a friend, and we all had been clueless.

I decided to reach out and help Jeff get these words into a book. Jeff's jail-written notes are rough, tumbled, and jumbled. They came from him as they needed, and I wanted to keep this feeling for readers, so be patient if you're trying to find that linear timeline in this story – it's not there. Rather, the text is Jeff's regurgitation of experiences, memories and reflections that needed to be written down on paper as part of his recovery path.

I hope you enjoy The Amazing Tragic and pass Jeff's story to others, so they can be inspired by his recovery from such a deep and dark place.

Tim Richter, Editor

Preface

This is a memoir that was written while I was an inmate at the Orange County Jail in Goshen, NY, between August 27th and September 18th, 2017. It is dedicated to my girlfriend and my two children. I want to thank them for giving me a life worth living and saving me from myself.

Above all I want to thank God for rescuing me from certain death and helping me see how sick I was. I also want to thank my deceased father, and my father-in-law. These two men never gave up on me and had so much strength and dignity; I can only wish to attain that level of living.

I want to thank my mother. Without you, I would have been doing half of my life behind bars. You saved my ass so many times and helped me in so many ways.

This story isn't written in any chronological order and it reads as a testament in the life of an addict. I hope you can find some wisdom and strength through these words.

May God bless and keep you always…

PEACE,
Jeffrey Bovee
St. Christopher's Inn 9/23/2017

Table of Contents

The Amazing Tragic

Nowhere Left to Go

It's 2017 and I'm sitting in the blazing hot August sun on a road-side exit ramp flying a sign that reads, "I'm homeless, broke, and looking for spare change." I've basically become a vagrant, living by the mercy of the good people who feel sorry for people like me and provide pity. I am 46 years old. I am a heroin and cocaine addict living in squalor in the city of Newburgh, New York, where cheap drugs afford me the luxury of getting through each day.

I made my way back to Newburgh after I initially touched down here in 2008 looking for crack before going to a family wedding. Back then, I was a methadone maintenance client and had a raging crack habit. Not much has changed except it's now ten years later and I'm living in a crack house around the corner from the dope spot. Everyone around here either sells drugs or does them so I'm in the perfect "worst" company.

My whole existence is down to the needle and the spoon and the stem. I need to feed my jones 3-4 times a day. I've been an addict of heroin, opiates, and cocaine since 1999 and it's been 20 years of extreme pain and false pleasure that only an addict would know. Like clockwork every morning, I need something to put in my veins just to get the gears turning.

The anxiety of not having my morning fix is incomprehensible. I develop the kind of skin crawling anxiety that just takes your breath away leaving me scared shitless if it's not available. I make sure that never happens, I won't let it get to that.

1

Jeffrey Bovee

I was living in Woodstock – a tiny and hip arts town in Ulster County, New York. I'm in Newburgh because, as an addict, it was virtually impossible for me to survive in Woodstock, even under employable situations. The latter hasn't been happening lately either. I learned how to survive by pan handling, a skill I picked up while I was touring on the road with The Grateful Dead back in the 1980s.

I had hitch-hiked around the country looking for something greater than myself and yearning to feel connected to something. Anything. Now, I'm using cocaine and heroin because it has become the center of my universe. I am unemployable, famished in every way, and wanted by the police. I can't get clean to save my life.

All of this changed rather suddenly when I was finally picked up on a warrant for stealing two bicycles from a Target store and blowing off court. I'm currently writing this story for you from the confines of my jail cell. The worst place to be? I'm certain it is, but I'm also thinking that God has a plan for me; at least I hope he does!

Every day before my arrest, I was going through the process of pan handling just enough money to support my $180/day cocaine and heroin habit. Whether I did it in front of a big box store, a street corner, or these highway ramps and exits didn't matter if I raised the funds to keep me right.

I prayed to God every day that people would be generous and pity me. It worked. It was degrading, and it often felt like a mission impossible. It was the only way to get what I needed when I wanted it and I wanted it now. All the money went to the dope man. Every cent. There is no camaraderie amongst drug users. Everyone lives for themselves and exists only to fulfill their own needs.

I never knew my life would take such a drastic turn for the worst, but I did hear the stories growing up. I made myself believe the lie that it could never happen to me. I looked like a skeleton and my mental health and spirit were in ruins. All the people that cared about me had turned their backs after years of me going in and out of treatments and jails.

I couldn't understand why they did this. I figured, if it was just drugs, why not give me a million chances at making it right again? Addiction is a disease? I couldn't grasp that concept either. I know it can be treated but when you're active and in the thick of it, you can't imagine it all coming to an abrupt end.

People get tired of all the bullshit you put them through. It's a fact. They hear the endless stream of lies like, "I can kick this on my own" or "I'm going to get help tomorrow". It never gets any better and you descend into the darkest void imaginable. The outcomes of active addiction are really sad. Addiction takes so much from you as a human being and leaves you empty and broken.

When you're locked up and become a prisoner you know you're going to be forced to go "cold turkey" and that is your worst nightmare. There are no freedoms or privileges, you just suck it up and hope for the worst of it to be over in 72 hours. It never is, that information is pure bullshit passed down amongst us dope fiends.

In Over My Head

My addiction to heroin and prescription opiates began in 1999. I was an alcoholic and cocaine addict playing in a band when I was first turned on to it. The opiates were cheap compared to the cost of my drinking episodes and when they entered my body my drinking completely disappeared. I lost my desire to drink as I once did.

The truth is I became addicted to anything and everything that I tried and liked. I was a bit naïve to the mechanics of the opiate scene but when the pill source dried up, I knew heroin was then the only way to relief. The heroin was strong and cheap back then, nothing like the garbage on the streets today that is killing people left and right. In the beginning I snorted everything, I was afraid of needles. I had a feeling I would like it too much and it scared me when I watched other people nodding out immediately after administration.

It also didn't take long before I noticed I was in over my head and shit started to get bad quick. I sold my belongings, wrote bad checks, stole from my family, and schemed my way through the dependency. I told far out stories on why all this was happening, but nobody believed a word I said. It comes with the territory. Looking back now, I couldn't hide anything except for that first year or so transitioning from alcohol to opiate addiction. The cat was out of the bag as they say, and things started to get very complicated as a result.

My family picked up on my problem after my second DWI arrest in 2001. I ended up being charged with a felony because I had a previous one in 1995. Two DWI's within ten years constitutes felony status in New

York State. I ended up with a sentence of five years' probation and a one thousand dollar fine. I was completely addicted to opiates by this time and kept it hidden from my probation officer and the substance abuse counselors. That deception alone felt like a full-time job.

The professional prying eyes afforded me enough rope to hang myself. Sadly, I ended up violating the terms and conditions of probation and was sent to the Ulster County Jail for a six-month sentence. I only made it a year on probation, so I hired a high-priced lawyer to get the remainder of it vacated.

This was a great deal at the time but would later come back to haunt me in future incarcerations when I could have received treatment. It did me no justice and the probation department made a mental note of it. My train had stopped briefly at the station and left at full speed ahead, barely staying on the track. The only good things happening were my new relationship and my creativity.

I was writing, recording, and performing with my band and started to get some notoriety. My relationship with my girlfriend, who is still my partner 18 years later, was a gift from God. More on that, later. The fact of the matter was I was an addict and I was far from entertaining the thought of cleaning up anytime in the distant future.

By 2001, I had been in three serious relationships and they were all long-term and all drug/alcohol-related to varying degrees. Everything from here on out in my life was fueled, destroyed, and rebuilt under the influence of narcotics. I was a thirty-one-year-old man, but I was living like I was invincible, hard and fast. I didn't care much about anything but drugs, although I tried my hardest to meet the needs of my loved ones.

The writing was on the wall and I chose not to read the memo. I should have seen it coming because I used to go to any length to procure marijuana when I was a twelve-year-old kid. I kind of knew I would have trouble. I just never thought I would end up in jails and institutions. Even as I write this from my jail cell, I have yet to figure out what really fueled my addiction. I'm hoping by the time I'm done here writing this I will have found out.

I come from the classic divorced family, but other than that, and zero supervision, my childhood wasn't that different than most. I was never beaten or abused, I was just left to my own devices and grew up way to fast. It was unchartered territory then and I still feel like I'm searching for direction now. I was an adult before I was a teenager. It was the classic case of wanting to get where I wanted to go without any hindrances. My brother turned me on to marijuana for the first time at the ripe old age of eleven.

I sit here contemplating all that has caused destruction and holds weight, I ask God for guidance. Right now, there is nobody out there left to help. Everyone is gone - I had a fleeting feeling this would eventually happen. Being a two-time felon incarcerated over six times in county and state facilities means all the rules have changed. At this point I'm doing all I can in this cell to just not hurt myself.

I'm distraught beyond belief and when your brain doesn't make those natural feel good chemicals anymore it's a wrap. There is nothing left to jump start anything that resembles joy except for the drugs that destroyed me. These transmissions inside our brains can take months and even years to return to balance. I'm ten days into detox and ready to just call it a day and give up on my life.

I just can't see or feel any hope or positivity in anything. I'm trying so hard to pray for forgiveness for all the wrongs and transgressions. It feels like my head is ready to explode and being estranged from my family and freedom has disconnected me from everything I thought I cherished.

Here is the beginning of another chapter in the life of a junkie whose world has been turned upside down. This is another sad story in the life of addiction, a real-world story that is going to hopefully free me from the prison in my head. Let us begin.

Beginnings

I was born Jeffrey Michael Bovee on October 4th,1970. I was a huge 10 pounds 12 ½ oz. baby and I remember throughout my life my mom saying I ruined her body. I knew from early on I was a bit odd and different because I used to be a rocker and liked to bang my head into my pillow while listening to music. I had zero supervision from as early as I can remember, and my folks worked split shifts.

I was smoking cigarettes at five years old when my brother and the other older neighborhood kids would walk me out of grocery stores with cigarette cartons down my pants. I lived on Pine Street in Kingston, NY and back then it wasn't the bad area it is today. My folks were young and used to fight a lot. I always wondered why they even were married and had kids because they just couldn't get along.

My older brother was five years older than me and started getting in trouble at a very early age. My little sister was three years younger than me and was always in the shadows of everything. My folks separated and divorced by the time I was five years old and it was a violent and drawn out clash of personalities and values - the kind of friction and fighting no kid should see or be exposed to. All I can say is by the time they made it to court and we were pushed and pulled back and forth, we all ended up in the custody of my dad.

I was five years old and I shut down inside, I didn't know what to make of the new arrangements. The little supervision I used to have completely went out the window as a result of these changes in the family dynamic. Everything seemed surreal and strange. I didn't know where I fit in and I was a quiet introverted little guy. I started to act strange, but nobody seemed to notice. My sister began her journey as the lost child and my brother became my dad's best buddy and hero. I remember being out at night, sometimes by myself till 10 PM, just wandering the streets of my neighborhood until my dad would send my brother out to get me. Or, I would hear my dad yelling on the front porch for me.

It seemed that my parents didn't realize what kids were facing and struggling with, because I believe they blocked it all out. A defense mechanism of sorts to hide the fact they were less then available than they should be. I guess they figured we were old enough to express ourselves, take care of ourselves, and know right from wrong by default. I learned more from being a silent observer and from the street then I did from my own parents, it was a scary time for me then.

I needed discipline and guidance. I received none and I never blamed my folks. I just ran with it like it was completely normal. When my folks finalized the divorce in 1975, I remember the next couple of years being very difficult and uncertain. Eventually, my dad remarried a younger lady and we all moved as a family up to Claremont, New Hampshire in New England. I started second grade up there and it was major culture shock, being a kid from New York.

We moved into a smaller house on Maple Avenue, a few blocks down from my new school. I made friends quickly, adjusted accordingly, and came to love and embrace my new life up there. Even after we left Claremont and moved farther north up to Haverhill, NH, it was just a great state to live in and easy for me to adapt. I loved New England life, it was laid back, safe, and supportive with great friends and wonderful caring families on every street.

While in Claremont, my brother started getting in trouble and was experimenting with alcohol and marijuana. This started a trend for him that would wreak havoc on our family unit. I tried to pay no attention and do my own things like a kid should, but the fighting between my folks over his behavior often got nasty. By the time my dad and step-mom had their own child, I was ten, my bro was fifteen, and my sister was seven. We would come to take a back seat because of the new addition to our family, but I loved her, and it was nice to have the focus off me. This was the most normal family life I ever had. That spoke volumes to me especially after the trauma of the divorce and losing my mom as a result.

Life in New England for me was like a dream; I was surrounded by nature and excelled in sports. I had many friends and my family life was stable. I was feeling like this was finally the ideal life I was searching for and I was just happy for the first time. When word came from my father that he was taking a new job further north and we would be moving, I was crushed. It felt like being chopped down to size, small and insignificant all over again.

It was bad enough that I only saw my real mom on holiday visits to New York and rarely spoke to her on the telephone. I loved my stepmother very much for the stability she brought our family and the discipline she instilled in us, but it was a lot to process and it was too little, too late for me. I never called her mom and I know that affected her, up until she bore her own child with my dad. The family dynamic just changed and we kind of dissipated into our own little worlds.

I understand these changes now, but as a kid I wasn't prepared emotionally to deal with or talk about them. I did have fleeting notions that holding everything in would cause me trouble, but I was so worried about being abandoned again that I sucked it up and plowed along. I felt like no one cared about my feelings and, although I knew my dad did his very best to anchor our family, he worked too much to be available on the level I required. My dad and stepmom went out on the town often, enjoying themselves as much as possible.

I remember alcohol being something my father enjoyed. Sometimes a little too much. I remember this because he would always be in a good mood and then the following day, he would be laid up in bed not wanting anyone to bother him. Mostly, I spent a lot of weekends at friend's houses. I was trying to get to know myself as best as I could. I watched out for my little sister, because she was just a young kid living completely unnoticed in the background of this family. When I look back now, I wonder how she escaped addiction.

The first time I ever put a drink or drug in my system I was an eleven-year-old kid. I stole beers out of my grandfather's fridge down in his basement. Pabst Blue Ribbon was the poison and I loved how it made me feel right away. It wasn't long after that I smoked marijuana with my older brother. The classic case of peer pressure, but I embraced it as a natural chain of events.

I'll never forget that evening, Pink Floyd "Wish You Were Here" on eight-track, the room dark with just the lights of the stereo on, the sweet aromatic smell of the weed burning in the air. My brother's first words as he passed it to me were, "Don't be a pussy. Hit that thing - it won't hurt you." I didn't know if I was going to be able to handle it and I certainly was worried about it making me sick, but I did it anyway. From there on out I became a regular pot smoker.

For me, smoking seemed natural. It was scary, and I got high, but it was fairly mild that first time. When I entered seventh grade junior high school, I was doing it every chance I could. I was stealing alcohol from home and bringing it to the school grounds. Music, partying, and experimenting with drugs became my calling. I hung out with people who were into the same thing as me and we would utilize every opportunity we could to hang out and do our thing. I look back now and see that I was just a kid; my brain hadn't even fully developed. I was totally and utterly uninformed of the dangers and it wouldn't be long till trouble would crop up.

The Middle Years

The year is 1980! And I'm ten years old and my family is in our last years of living in New Hampshire. My dad took a gamble on a job with a new newspaper up north in Haverhill in the Connecticut River valley and it turned into a bust. I think we were there for about a year. We lived in a brand-new trailer in a trailer park before we lost everything and had to move back to New York. It was the first time in my life I noticed how important money was to a family and we were on the balls of our ass as they say. The trailer was sent ahead to New York and we settled into my stepmother's folk's house, where I picked up my first drink.

I started sixth grade at Anna Devine Elementary in Rifton, NY, and we eventually settled into a trailer park on River Road in Tillson, in late 1981. My life and the life of my family was about to go through some major upheaval upon our return to the Empire state. It was a gamble with a losing hand. All manner of weirdness and even stranger occurrences were about to manifest themselves. I started my alcohol and drug use here at the ripe age of eleven and Tillson would become a hotbed of activity for sex, drugs, and rock n roll. It's where I earned my stripes and although I was yet to become a casualty, the early days proved exciting and adventurous.

This new environment is where I noticed my taste for psychedelics and I took many acid trips up in the mountains off Springtown Rd. The world was in the beginning of the "Ronald Reagan Years" and life was about to become one long strange trip that I had no control over.

I don't think my brother had any clue just how damaging and dangerous drugs were to himself or to me. I believe he was looking to me as a companion in his own journey of experimentation. He is five years older than me, so he had a head start on me and knew a little bit about drinking and getting stoned. I was just a kid and had no clue of the shit I was about to embark on, but I can tell you this, it grabbed me up hard and fast and I didn't have a chance. All the insecurities and unresolved childhood issues on top of the lack of supervision created the perfect storm for me to get swept up in.

I was still reeling from leaving our beautiful haven in New Hampshire. Here we were, back in New York being exposed to some things I couldn't escape from. The progression I went through in hindsight was just mind blowing but living back then it seemed like I would never grow old. I became a teenager faster than my brain had time to develop. The peer pressure was way too much for me to handle, and the parenting was sketchy at best.

I became exposed to things that, as a kid, would mold and shape me forever. The days of innocence were over from here on out. All I wanted was to be an adult. I never even remotely entertained being a kid anymore. Being a kid was for chumps, I was a big boy now. This would be a life choice that forced me to endure a lot of pain.

I entered Myron J. Michael middle school in 1983 in Kingston, NY. I immediately met my new best friend, and partner in crime and many other endeavors. The guilty party was a kid from Yonkers, NY. He lived in Port Ewen, a small town on the Hudson River. We enjoyed the exact same things like a deep genuine love of art, music, writing, and trouble. We created a little squad of buddies who we got high and drunk with on a regular basis, we were inseparable, and we became like brothers. We are still close today but like all good things they changed and mutated. You take separate roads and hope they converge again but they rarely do.

My life as a teenager immediately became problematic, because I felt insignificant all over again. I wasn't handsome enough, cool enough, or popular enough for my own good. I covered up all these emotions with the drugs and the lifestyle. By the time I turned fourteen I had used pot, coke, speed, benzos, acid, and mushrooms. I fell in love with all the old classic rock bands and tried to live according to them, especially my new favorite band The Grateful Dead. My best friend and I made it a point to start our own band Mad Hatter that mirrored the psychedelic experience we loved so much. This was the birthing period of my musical development. We searched out people exactly like us and went about to change the world.

I spent hours upon hours listening, practicing, and dedicating my life to music and writing. It became my calling, my purpose; it's all I ever wanted to do. I wrote poetry, songs, prose, and observations. My days were spent creating, getting high, hanging out with friends, and spending as much time as I could in nature. Things quickly began to fall apart in school because I couldn't concentrate, and I never wanted to be there and put the work in.

The first trouble I experienced was when I was fourteen in the summer before ninth grade. I got hooked up with some delinquent friends. They turned out to be thieves – we went to the trailer where my mom and her boyfriend lived to steal some weed. We started rooting through the house and found an ounce of high-grade cocaine. I ended up taking it and disappeared for a week. I don't remember much else, but I know I didn't sleep for a week and ended up in a severe cocaine depression and crash.

My mom and everyone else were worried sick that I was dead somewhere. I wasn't allowed at my Mom's anymore. Her boyfriend was a user like me and I violated him and their home. I had been taking their stash all along but was always careful not to let them notice. There was always weed, hash, alcohol, and pills lying around and plenty of it at that.

The collateral damage was my mom and her boyfriend's relationship ending as well as my dad and stepmother's marriage, also. They all had enough and were blown away that I was using drugs. After dealing with my older brother's problems, they weren't prepared for something of this magnitude to occur. My mom moved out of her boyfriend's place, and my stepmother filed for divorce from my father.

The only good thing to come out of all this trouble was my dad and my mom became close again. They were only friends again, but it was nice to have them on speaking terms, communicating, and helping one another heal after I destroyed the relationships with my actions. Back then I always gravitated to older people; I was exposed to things as a teenager completely in an adult league.

When I was fifteen is when I was able to attend my first Grateful Dead show. The shows were November 10th and 11th at the Brendan Byrne arena in East Rutherford, NJ. A whole bunch of us went down for the weekend and stayed in a hotel. We were taking a lot of acid back then and it was a rite of passage for us deadheads. My own band, Mad Hatter, was evolving rapidly and we catered to the deadheads and Pink Floyd fans with our excursions into the psychedelic realms. We were the pioneers of acid rock in the 1980s and thoroughly into the pudding as they say. During those times I was still finding my way and still felt insecure and unsure of myself and the world around me. I just didn't always feel comfortable in my own skin or head and I utilized psychedelic experiences, "trips," to get outside of myself.

Inadequate is a term I can use to describe how I felt especially with the women. I did lose my virginity at thirteen, but I had no clue what the hell I was doing sexually. I knew I gravitated to a certain type of woman, but it was elusive, and they were far more experienced and older than me most of the time. It was hard to express myself and I always fumbled with my words and advances.

At sixteen, I behaved like an adult and went about my life in the fast lane approach to everything. Looking back now I feel like I lost my childhood. All the good clean fun was incognito. Keg parties, acid eating, pot smoking, and women chasing was all I wanted to do. Music and writing were the only wholesome and normal things I took part in and I did them under the influence, too. The group of people I hung out with did all the same things I did, and school was a breeding ground for these activities. Free thinking and heavy partying, school skipping, and house parties, acid trips in nature and away from home was how I survived.

My band started getting a lot of gigs and we used to turn them into acid parties and the alcohol flowed like a river. Life seemed like it was in a flux where nothing grew old and I never entertained the idea of a future beyond what I was engaged in. Good times and filling my cup up to the rim was the order of the day. All this fun started to catch up with me in school and my average quickly dropped and my appearances at the dean's office increased. The teachers were all onto me, but I managed to get around that by being under the radar as much as possible.

I could do the work when I wanted to, but I missed so many days it started to catch up and showed a pattern of behavior they couldn't and wouldn't endorse. The reasons for me missing school were elaborate and unbelievable. They began to question my home life and I always had to be one step ahead of the faculty. I intercepted the mail and never brought home a report card. The only reason I even got away with it was because it was just my dad and brother at home and he worked too much. He tried in the beginning to hold me accountable, but it was impossible for a single parent like my dad to stop a locomotive like me.

Live & Learn

At seventeen, right before Christmas vacation in my eleventh-grade year of school I was finally kicked out of school for good. I was truant way too much and the staff and teachers were just plain tired of putting up with my lack of respect to rules. The dean, the principal, psychiatrist, and superintendent decided for me that I was going to finish school at night and get my GED. During the day I would work at a fast food Chinese restaurant. My father laid down the law that if I was no longer a student and wanted to be treated like an adult, I would have to pay rent to live under his roof and get the diploma pronto.

I left home as much as possible, staying wherever I could do my own thing. After everything broke down at school, my relationship with my family changed even more. I had already ruined two relationships in my family and when my dad started to date a woman half his age, it became his total focus. He sure the hell wasn't going to let me fuck this one up!

My sister had moved in with my mom. She hadn't lived with her since she was three years old. I know it must have been extremely hard on her, but she was a trooper. My sister escaped addiction to drugs but there were some mental health issues because of the family dynamics. My brother had been living in Florida and New York City and I don't remember him being around that much. He would appear and disappear randomly whenever things got tough or money got tight. My brother managed to never get jammed up like me, not even close.

Anyway, around this time I was hitchhiking everywhere to get where I needed to go. I just put my thumb out and let God do the rest. I was surviving, and I had a strong constitution, but I also had a rebellious attitude towards society's principals.

The story of my life as an addict has always been about getting off easy and finding the easiest, softest path without consequences. It's always been about getting what I want, when I want it, and whatever it takes to get it. I always want it now and I always made certain that I never went without. If it meant I had to lie, cheat you, or steal, I did whatever was needed to survive. By the time I was sixteen going on seventeen, I had already lived as an active drug user for five years.

Back then in the 80s I had never heard of treatment. Detox and rehab were terms I wouldn't entertain for another ten long years. It's strange, the progression. It sneaks up on you and then it feels like you missed the bus, that you're way too late. You never see the trouble coming. It invades every space of your psyche and by the time it rears its pointed little head, turning around isn't an option.

Two more friends entered the picture in 1986-1987, the Joker and Fitz. These two guys were a year or two ahead of me in high school and we became very close and good friends. We were like brothers - deadheads and road dogs that lived hard and fast and ingested copious amounts of LSD. We were huge fans of psychedelic music and the experience.

One of my great friends, lost her mind at a Grateful Dead show. She loaded a shotgun, put it in her mouth, and blew her head off to quiet the voices and pain she was experiencing. She had just escaped from the psych ward. She was eighteen years old, an artist with immense talent, and an incredible singer.

It was a gut wrenching and horrible display of the power drugs have on a young person. She is buried in a nearby cemetery. I go there often and speak to her, but it isn't any easier dealing with it now as it was then. I think I vowed to stop taking acid, but I didn't, I probably just made sure I didn't take copious amounts out of fear of joining her with the same fate. God bless and keep you always. You were one of the good ones who left us too soon.

The next big change came when my dad and his new girlfriend moved to an apartment complex in the city of Kingston around 1988. My best friends and I turned it into the hangout spot and set it up with a psychedelic lightshow and sound system. My buddies and I were very close, and we use to go on all kinds of crazy adventures on acid. We bonded on all those trips and when the call came to move to California, my new friend, the Joker took the bait. I was devastated to lose him, but I made my own plans to link up with him via the summer of 1989 Grateful Dead tour.

I was so excited to travel out west, it felt like a soul calling. It was another rite of passage for any deadhead out there. The great American road adventure. Plus, there were the drugs! The West Coast. Ground zero for the psychedelic experience and bands that I loved. It felt like I was finally going home, or at least that is what I thought at the time. There're so many significant players, friends, band mates, and drug buddies that it's difficult to call everyone out. They were all special people who touched my life in various ways, sometimes good, sometimes bad. The problem with name checking everyone throughout this story is the involvement and unspoken hierarchy of our highness.

We all suffered great and small losses, and some none at all. Most of us came from low to middle class families and the ones who were rich, were generous and always had the good stuff, if you know what I mean. We all have our own stories to tell, it's hard enough now being a 46-year-old man locked down in a jail cell, estranged from his family, trying to make sense of all the misadventures.

I can't stress enough the importance the 80s played in my future addiction development. Everything was so new and exciting and without consequence. The first times were endless, and it was "you had to be there" type shit. My feelings were full of wonder and that far out independence that a lot of us experience in the beginning. I still did my best to block out all the insignificant feelings, not knowing what I wanted out of life. That world, my world, was just a microcosm of an altered state of consciousness in a mind that hadn't matured properly. I felt a foreboding sometimes - the trips showed me so much truth it could be scary.

I quickly learned how to pretend not to see or feel anything that would jeopardize my journey. As the second half of the 80s began, things started to become very complicated. There were issues I figured out early that were truth. My love of music, nature, and writing were the foundation that stick out as holding some weight. I am a writer, musician, and I have a deep love for nature even today after all the pain and trouble.

In hindsight, sitting here at this filthy wooden desk surrounded by concrete and steel, it's quite scary and disturbing going over a life that got away from you. Life ebbs and flows, but the current carrying you downstream never falters or changes course. You're either minding the store or everything is being looted right from under your nose.

Everything back home was on hiatus. My new girlfriend, who I started dating, waited for my return from California. My band also took a break because this particular Dead tour was of the utmost importance amongst all of us. Most people didn't think I would return or make it back in one piece. I was a casualty to them without even knowing it myself. People always looked at me as pushing the envelope. I remember as the tour out west wrapped up that California wasn't going to be kind to me on a financial level, so I left my buddy the Joker and headed up to Oregon with the stragglers.

It became apparent that my West Coast adventure was at its natural end and I decided to hitchhike back to New York. Four thousand miles, totally broke, eighteen years old, and a long way from home. I called for a rescue mission back home from my folks in the form of a Greyhound ticket and was told flat out to figure it out on my own. Tough love was the order served up on my request, so I sucked it up and planned out my journey back east. I couldn't even fathom them leaving me out there like that, but they did. I guess they figured I was strong and smart enough to get back safely.

I was scared as I made my way to the interstate to begin the journey. I headed out on 80 east between Washington and Oregon along the Columbia River Valley. I knew this was the only way to get back home and I said to myself, "I can do this." I traveled for five long days and sleepless nights. I was on the asphalt under a hot August sun and ended up dumping half of my belongings I started out with.

Some of the trip was easy because truckers took me about half way across in long legs, but some of it was painstaking and hard on the head. When I finally rolled into Kingston, NY, going through the NYS Thruway toll booth, I realized I just did the unthinkable.

All my friends and family were amazed I made it back in one piece. When I arrived home to my mom's house her first contact with me was opening my bedroom door and seeing me vomit into an ashtray because I was already drunk. Pretty disturbing stuff for sure!

My girlfriend and I were reunited along with my band and all my friends. My first girlfriend was great because she was a buffer between my folks and me. My mom really liked her because she was a naturalist, quiet and unassuming, the opposite of my mom. She was more of a friend and partner in crime then someone I was madly in love with. I did love her, but I think I loved the fact I had a caretaker and someone who cared about me more than anything.

We both loved alcohol and psychedelics and took a lot of acid trips together. You form a bond with people you trip with because it naturally creates that interconnectedness especially when you're at the peak of the experience. The psychological effect is questionable, but there is something there that happens and it sure the hell feels like you're in tune with everything and everyone around you. For the next 5-6 years we played house together and went through a lot. It was a relationship that couldn't last forever but I held on because I was afraid of change and abandonment never fit me well.

1989 ended with our annual New Year's Eve show at The Modena Madhouse, a fraternity house outside New Paltz, NY. Mad Hatter always played on New Year's Eve, just like the Grateful Dead. We were a great and special band. Never before, or after, did I have a camaraderie as tight and developed as that band. The first band you work in always holds an extra special place in your heart and soul. Those cherished memories contrasted the harsh realities of people lost along the way, acid casualties who never came back.

Writing this memoir reminds me of how much work I put into my craft, even as I sit in this jail cell pouring over the pages, I remind myself how important my work is to me. It was my calling at age thirteen and continues to this day regardless of the circumstances.

ODs, OPs, & Homelessness

On September 27, 2015, I was at my home in the town of Woodstock, NY. I had been using prescription opiates like Dilaudid and Oxycodone, but I would also chip away at heroin whenever possible and I was getting ready for a crash landing in a magnitude I would never forget. There was a particularly strong and lethal batch of heroin on the streets of my area called "White Zombie" and it was incapacitating in small doses. My dealer had warned me and my running buddy Daniel that "White Zombie" had knocked a few people out, but I didn't pay much attention to his warnings. I had been using heroin off and on since 1999 and I never once overdosed. I was sure it could never happen to me. I was very wrong.

That day, I had visited my father's grave and then went to purchase some dope before heading home. I was downstairs in my living room and my girlfriend was upstairs showering and my youngest boy was on the couch sleeping. I loaded a needle up in the dark, not paying attention to how much I put out and went in the bathroom to take the shot. I barely made it out of the bathroom and fell into the garbage can in the hallway. The next thing I remember is coming too like a lightning bolt.

I was hooked up to IV's and a breathing apparatus. The EMTs had revived me with Narcan and a shot of adrenaline into my heart. I came to, thinking I was dying when in fact I had been saved. The EMTs tried to calm me down and get me breathing on my own. That jolt ripped me from a near-death experience – it was extremely surreal. Another few minutes and I would have been dead.

Jeffrey Bovee

My girlfriend was crying hysterically, and it took a long time for the neural pathways in my brain and the muscle coordination to come back to a balance. I was shaking uncontrollably like I was having a seizure and it felt at that moment like I did something permanently destructive to my brain. They loaded me onto the stretcher and wheeled me out of my house into a cold September night with the prying eyes of my neighbors watching from their windows.

I was on the way to the hospital with my first overdose hanging over me like a dark luminous cloud of contempt. I continued to have the sensation of being submerged underwater and I couldn't get warm or stop shaking. The event scared the living shit out of me. It was too horrifying to grasp, and I now saw, firsthand, how fragile life really is. I didn't want to die and leave my family distraught, but I also wasn't ready to stop using, even after almost losing my life.

I was able to get back on my replacement medicine, Suboxone, but I knew in my heart I wanted to get another fix when things cooled down. The Ulster County Child Protective Services arrived at my home after I was discharged from the hospital. The staff at the hospital reported me because a child was present in the house at the time of the overdose. They launched a lengthy and thorough investigation into my life. My family and I were put under the microscope with intense scrutiny. I had my doctor and therapist in my corner to aid in my defense, but the chief investigator was trying to have me removed from the household.

I don't know how I made it through the investigation, but I pulled strings and manipulated my way through it. I utilized the right sympathetic people including a therapist I got onboard that I knew from High School. I coordinated everything just right to paint a picture of a patient who stopped taking his meds and had a relapse. I tried my hardest to make it look like an unfortunate one-off event. It was a classic case of a slip and I would pull my faculties back together and plow on clean and sober. It was the farthest thing from the truth and I was in major denial protecting my use like it was more important than anything else in this world.

Nothing was going to take me out of the game, I was headed down a very dark path and I didn't really entertain staying clean at all. After the overdose and subsequent consequences, I did start to take my medicine properly. But it didn't take long before I was back to selling my script and using the funds to finance my illegal opiate habit. My family suffered as much or more as a result of my behavior, but I just let them carry on and ignored all the signs of the downward spiral my life had become.

I disappeared to the safe house downtown with my man and stuck needles in my arm like I never missed a beat. The worst was yet to come, and the bottoms became deeper and more pronounced. I started a journey that wouldn't end until everything precious to me would be taken away.

Three months after the overdose, I was back to being a full-blown heroin addict. I was also hitting the prescription opiates. I would steal from my dealer's house whenever he would leave it unattended. I would steal anything and everything if it had value and wasn't bolted down or locked up tight. At home I wasn't contributing to my family's welfare and security and was in debt way over my head with my employer.

My vehicle was always on assorted drug runs and I was running it into the ground. It seemed like there was nothing to stop me from all the running around I was doing. I knew the risks and consequences because they all happened before. I just ignored all the signs and kept it moving because I was on a mission. I was the devil's right-hand man and I would do whatever I wanted. I forgot the people who depended on me.

I couldn't function as a writer or singer/songwriter. I flunked performances in my band. Everyone saw the writing on the wall but staged no interventions. I believe they were so used to these activities in the past that they just figured why bother he's going to end up locked up.

This time, the run was completely destroying everything in its path and, as my desperation increased, odds of getting out unscathed fell towards zero.

Detox after detox was how the year 2017 began. I think I went to five sessions between January and March. I was seeking the quick fix to appease my family and friends. There was no light at the end of the tunnel and dark and heavy clouds were looming on the horizon. Trouble was brewing and bubbling just beneath the surface. I was doing all the wrong things, expecting different results. It was the pure definition of insanity.

By the time March had arrived, it had been a long, lonely, and destructive winter. The holidays had been ruined by my drug use and nobody trusted me. There was no glimmer of hope that I would change and get help anytime soon. I would like to think my girlfriend and children believed in me, but they were just putting on a brave face.

My oldest son was old enough to know there was something wrong with his Dad because of how I was moving. He always would say "I just want you to get better." It's all everyone wanted. No one could bear to see me in this state - I was slowly killing myself.

Understandably, my own mother wanted nothing to do with me after I had called her a cunt on Christmas Day. I was in a rage and let her have it because she told me I ruined another holiday. I have tried to reach her here from jail, but she refuses my calls. My mom is all about tough love and being on the opposite end of it can feel very sad and lonely.

The day of March 27, 2017 is when my world changed, and crash landed around me. I was taking my girlfriend to work. She could tell I was acting strange and something wasn't right. I hadn't taken enough shots that day and I was in a hurry to get to my dealer for a package to take home. I couldn't wait to drop her off and get to the house and take a shot before my kids arrived home from school.

I drove like mad to the dope man and sped home in time to get everything in order to get straight. It's always an issue because the first thing you learn as a junkie is you're always waiting on the man. He's never early, he's always late. I dropped him $100 and made it clear that I was going to make the first one count because I was in withdrawal.

I'll never forget that day as long as I live. My girlfriend pleads with me before I dropped her off to not do anything stupid. I did what every junkie does - I became the yes man to appease her worries.

"Don't worry, I'm fine. Nothing wrong here," I would say!

How wrong I would turn out to be. Injecting heroin of any kind is like playing Russian roulette. It destroys anything and everything in its path including your soul. The heroin I purchased that day was a particularly powerful batch and my dealer forgot to warn me that I didn't need much to get off. I had a $100 worth and dumped half of it in the spoon when I arrived home to take a shot.

I was pretty high, but I managed to be coherent enough to get my kids off the bus and settled in at home. Somehow, I managed to feed them, bathe them, do their homework, and get them settled in for the evening. The fact of the matter was I rushed them through the whole process so I could head into the bathroom to shoot up what was left.

At about 9:30 PM, I went into my upstairs bathroom and dumped the rest of my stash in the spoon and drew it up into the needle. I did my shot, threw everything in the garbage and that's all I remember.

Why I felt the need to do it all in one shot I really don't recall. I might have just wanted to get it in me and deal with getting more the next day. I walked out of the bathroom and collapsed into unconsciousness. I woke up disoriented with uniforms all around me. They were trying to save my life, again.

My oldest son heard me hit the floor and called 911. He performed CPR on me until the EMTs arrived with the police in tow. They got me back to breathing and sat me on the toilet with some oxygen. When you come out of an overdose your brain is all scrambled and you feel like your submerged under something very heavy.

When I finally got my wits I panicked and asked, "Where are my kids?!?" The police informed me they were safe and that my girlfriend was on her way to get them. Then they asked me, "Where are the drugs?"

I told them I had nothing, and the needle was buried in the garbage because I always throw everything out after I use. At that very moment I knew my life was about to change forever. The slap on the wrist stuff was no longer going to apply. I'll never forgive or forget what I did that night to my family, it still haunts me today. They loaded me up into the ambulance and rushed me to the hospital for evaluation.

The doctors and paramedics informed Child Protective Services that I was neglectful to my children and the whole curtain fell. I was also charged with two counts of endangering the welfare of a child. After I returned home from the hospital, I was ordered to vacate the premises and sign my custodial rights over to my girlfriend. I was further ordered to present myself to The Family Court of Ulster County.

My days of flying under the radar were over. I was homeless and had no resources to help me figure out my next move. I decided to check back into another detox at Cornerstone of Rhinebeck. I picked that place because that's where I always went for a quick fix and resume the ongoing war with myself. I did my five days and checked out, so I could get back to work. I needed funds from my boss to further fuel my addiction. I stayed in motels, friend's houses, and in tents. I had no intention of stopping now, especially being removed from my family. All I had done was to put a bandage on my brain. I was the same. My life was in ruins. I couldn't see outside of my own sick mental health and it was the beginning of the end for me. I was waging a war I would never win, and I just couldn't let my defenses down.

Decade of Decadence

The 90s were the decade when I went through an extreme amount of changes on every level. I endured so many heartaches and struggles that I barely came out alive. It was the decade where I started living at an alarming rate - fast and furious as they say. My alcoholism and drug addictions were waging a war against me; I felt I could never win, and I got smacked around and beaten down every step of the way.

Relationships started and ended. Old friendships collapsed, and new ones came out of the wood work. The 90s are the years when I was really on my own. I escaped a lot of damage by returning to the anchor of my mom's home when I was beaten down, shit got real in my twenties. Even with my family support, I should have lost my life dozens of times. I changed in ways that were irreversible.

There was a sense of danger and destruction that wasn't there in the 80s. I reached out to a lot of older people as mentors. They showed me how to survive in the hard drug culture. I was going through a learning curve of this new world and I wasn't even in tune with where I was coming from. This story is about to take a wrong turn and become dark.

The year 1990 was especially exciting in the sense that the Grateful Dead tours were brilliant. I was enamored with the hippie drug culture and the spring and summer runs across the East and Midwest were some of the best concerts that I ever saw. After summer ended, Brent Mydland, the band's keyboard player, died of an accidental overdose of morphine and cocaine commonly known as a speedball.

I saw his last show in Chicago - it wasn't the first nor the last time I would hear of overdoses amongst musicians. It was a sad day for my favorite band and they never fully recovered from the loss. Rather than recognize the danger of overdose, I thought "What is it about this heroin stuff that musicians love so much?" It would be five more years before I tried it, but this event perked my interest deep in my subconscious brain. By 1990, heroin was starting to make footholds in communities outside of big cities, kind of like the crack epidemic in the 80s.

In 1990 I was playing a lot of music, drinking tons of alcohol, and living life in the present as a young man who still didn't have a clue about a future much less a career. I guess I trained myself early on to believe it would work itself out on its own. What I came to find out was that I was at the mercy of the clock and that unmercifully kept on ticking. The seasons came and went and before I knew it decades were flying by. Everything is always happening, moving forward relentlessly, and I barely paid attention because I thought I was having fun.

The 1990s were my years of changing ethics, the feel-good vibe I had through being in the deadhead community of "love your brother" wasn't as important to me anymore. The alcohol really started to wear me down, but it was soothing the frayed connections in my brain from all those years of taking acid and other psychedelics. I would act out irrationally, violently, and dangerously. It was your typical Jekyll and Hyde syndrome, I could be extremely warm and happy, and terrifying at the same time depending on the amount I consumed and the surrounding environment. My relationships really started to unravel quickly.

In 1993, my girlfriend and I were near the end of our six-year relationship and I told myself I just didn't care. I was far from strong enough to be alone, but something told me I would be better off without her. I searched for alternative ways to calm my nerves, but my alcoholism was just numbing me and my feelings more and more. The drink was turning my life upside down.

I was in new surroundings as bars became my preferred place to be. The band I started in high school, Mad Hatter, had broken apart and my relationship was deteriorating, and I was starting to indulge in behavior that was risky and outside my comfort zone. I started to pick up different interests and joined some heavier rock bands with older people I met through drinking and partying. I went through so many changes in those first few years of the 90's it was monumental.

I grew my hair out super long and started to dress sharper, leaving the hippie clothing behind. I did a drastic makeover to fit in with how I felt - distinguished but drunken. I started to like the darker side of the street and hooked up with gutter punks, road dogs, dead end kids, workaholics, alcoholics, and hard drug users. Everything changed over so fast I barely realized I was setting myself up for a major change that would be hard to undo. My relationship ended and I didn't care about her or myself. I just needed to be medicated and drunk and everything was ok.

Without a girlfriend, I became a hedonistic, drunken, womanizing freak. My consumption was alarming to everyone and people started to back away from me. I was running the streets and bars partying until I passed out, so I didn't have to think. I retreated to my mom's house in Port Ewen, NY, a ranch-style house down the street from my favorite bar. My brother lived in the same town and being he was a heavy drinker we started to spend a lot more time together.

My life was a mess and I did nothing but continue to drown myself in the bottle. I was angry now that I lost my girl and did nothing to save the relationship. I started to see her around local watering holes with her new man and I would act belligerently and get violent. I didn't care anymore, people started to notice my lack of ability to function normally. I was interested in one thing and one thing only, drinking and taking drugs to the point of oblivion. I kept strange hours and even stranger bed fellows. I listened to extremely heavy music and wandered from bar to bar looking for people just like me.

I can't remember much more except I lost a lot of my old friends and liked to keep company with strangers. The women I met were all drunks and as soon as the sun rose, I disappeared as quickly as I met them. The days melted into one another and I was on the highway to hell, or hell in a bucket whichever got me there faster.

Starting in the early 1990s, I worked as a foreman in the t-shirt industry. Tie-dye t-shirts were huge during this time, especially as the Grateful Dead grew in popularity and everyone wanted one. I made tons of money through working in factories and taking on the responsibility of mixing the dye powders and coming up with creative designs. There was a lot of alcohol and drugs in the workplace, so I naturally fit right in - we were all addicts in one form or another.

At one point my girlfriend, my brother, and my sister all worked alongside of me because it was a big money maker. We indulged it. In the spring of 1993 after my relationship ended and my alcoholism was on the rise, I moved to an old church rectory on Wurts Street in downtown Kington, NY. It was a hulk of an old house with several bedrooms and endless space. It was the coolest party pad you could imagine. The rent was $600 a month plus utilities, but we had five people living in it. We all shared our alcohol and drugs and lived communally. It was a crazy scene night and day and the shit got out of control unbelievably quickly.

People came and went. There were always friends crashing on the couches or empty rooms. I lived there for a year and it coincided with the 1994 Woodstock festival at Winston Farm in Saugerties. About 400,000 people from all over the globe attended. The festival was three days of music, drugs, and heavy vibes. It rained like a bitch too turning the place into a sea of mud. I barely slept a wink and tripped for three days straight meeting and hanging out with friends and strangers.

When Woodstock was over, I returned to the house with my roommates. We had a transient population from California that we put up with for a few months because they had money to burn. I ended up becoming the designated drug runner for the household because I knew all the dealers downtown and crack was huge. I became seriously addicted to crack in only six months' time. I don't think I slept more than a few hours a day for those six months. I started to do things I never did before like writing bad checks, stealing shit, and lending my car out to the drug dealers. I could barely work and that included playing my music and writing. I was becoming a casualty and liability and there was no one to encourage positive behavior in anyway. We were all getting high and drinking like we weren't going to see tomorrow.

That area downtown was a hotbed for drug activity and gangs. It was the belly of the beast with raids happening all the time and cops were continuously patrolling the streets. I knew all the dealers because I went to school with most of them and the other guys were afraid to walk out the door into a predominantly black neighborhood. We were looked at like crazy white boys and they used to call me "Woodstock."

I became so incapacitated that my mom talked me into going to the hospital for help with my drinking and crack addiction. I was so messed up in the head, that the minute I stopped drinking and went to detox for the first time, they ended up locking me down in the psyche ward for thirty days because I had a violent psychotic episode and threatened the staff. They tied me down and shot me full of anti-psychotics and central nervous system depressants. I walked around for a week or so drooling on myself and shuffling up and down the halls. I even escaped once when they put me in a part of the hospital that wasn't locked down. I went downtown got so drunk I couldn't even walk and then came back the next day. From there on out they kept an eye on me and made sure I was in the secured area. I was there for thirty long days and then was shipped off to a rehab up in Amsterdam, NY for another thirty days of alcohol treatment.

It was 1995 and I was twenty-five years old. My addiction had finally got the best of me for the first time. That old saying of rehab ruining your using holds some weight because I was never the same after being exposed to a life of sobriety. It was my first experience and far from my last. I figured I was invincible and would get back to my normal routine just being more aware of how screwed up I could get if I didn't pay attention. I started right back when I got out and picked up my first DWI in 95 with a BAC of 0.27%, the cops told me I shouldn't even have been walking let alone driving. I refused the normal sobriety tests and just put my hands out and said take me in.

1995 was also the year the Grateful Dead came to an abrupt demise. Jerry Garcia, the fearless leader of the psychedelic nation, died in a rehab from complications to his health from decades of heroin and cocaine use. His body just couldn't handle the strain anymore and he had a heart attack in his sleep. I saw my last Dead shows that summer and I was shocked at how poor his health was. I was glad I went though, and my memories of those tours are priceless.

I want to stress that the 90s was full of lost days and nights and I'm having a tough time putting the pieces together in any kind of chronological order. The drug experience by nature is so bewildering and chaotic that there's no straightforward way to put it into a normal perspective.

Peaks and Valleys

1995-1996 were lost years for me. My alcoholism and crack cocaine use lead to my first hospitalization. After my release, I had a brief period of stabilization. I counted my losses and moved to my mom's house and began to put the pieces back together. My mother and father, who had divorced way back in 1975, bought a house together in the Town of Ulster, NY. It was a big, old townhouse in a little community and it was a perfect landing spot for me.

As soon as I could I moved in and started to concentrate on a normal routine. My dad, my mom, my sister, and I lived there together as a family. My brother had married and remained in his apartment over in Port Ewen. I actually pulled it together briefly, but by no means permanently. I was still drinking and getting high, but now I had to be crafty and aware of my intake.

All eyes were on me and it was tough to cut loose like the years before. I became a weekend warrior, mostly to just feel normal again. My nerves were frayed, and I couldn't get around the fact that my addiction had been found out. The labels and stigma were hard to shake off. Looking back now, the only thing that saved me from complete depression was my music and writing.

I dove into the creative world that I knew best. During the early 90s I was playing music in bands right up until my hospitalization. I played in funk bands and rock bands. I joined a duo of female musicians called Ivory Rose as part of their backup band. Ivory Rose became quite famous, playing big shows with national acts. I felt like I finally arrived, until I was booted for my alcohol and drug use.

I learned a valuable lesson then - I'm not the center of the universe. I began to see my alcoholism and drug addiction were robbing me of a good life, but I refused to change and do anything about it. I convinced myself it wasn't that bad, and I was having too much fun. I was just young, at that. It just wasn't in the cards yet and slowing down was enough of problem for me to handle.

Then the decade's second half began in earnest, so did my moments of delusion and grandeur. Life was about to take another turn, for better or worse. At the time it was questionable but complicated it would most certainly become. 1997-1998 were the two years that would change my life.

I was working as a foreman making tie-dye shirts with a friend that had started up a new factory. He was a fellow musician and deadhead. He took very good care of me financially for the next ten years under his employ. I was renting a house with friends on Albany Avenue in Kingston, NY. It had everything.

We held huge parties in the rehearsal space in the basement and it had four bedrooms for the rotating cast of addict friends. Many people would come and go even after I moved out and relinquished my role as caretaker, but it operated in the same way and catered to the same people. It was a party house and drug den.

Around this time, I met another woman, she was a bartender at my local watering hole and coke spot. I fell in love with her for all the wrong reasons. Everyone at the bar told me she only liked black men and was a bisexual, but I overlooked it as a minor inconvenience. It was all true, but I went with it and just said to myself I have to have this girl.

I had an inkling that she liked me, and we hooked up at a party at my house when she saw my band play for the first time. The relationship rooted so quickly I barely had time to process it. It was tumultuous, and I was extremely edgy and insecure in the beginning. I medicated myself with the usual substances, but she picked up on it and started to bother me about how much I drank and used. I cleaned up for her in the beginning but continued to sneak around and reward myself as often as possible.

I cared for her and tried to understand why she wanted me clean and sober, but it was a power play from the get-go. I was super confused because she resumed relations with other women and probably men too. Infidelity was in the mix and things started to get explosive. Our relationship was unhealthy, and it didn't have a chance in hell to grow. She was seven years younger than me and we were complete opposites in terms of interests. There was too much heartache and uncertainty and I felt like there was something better for me out there.

It took me awhile to get my bearings together when we decided to split up and she would walk in and out of my life even after we moved on. It was a cycle that was causing me a lot of emotional turmoil, because although we were together for a little over a few years, I knew she was never completely honest with me in the faithfulness department and I just wouldn't have it. There was a fair amount of drama as I looked for a new partner, and I can think of numerous times she would show up while I was out and about and make things hard on my head. She was untrustworthy, and I needed to get away from that kind of shit in the biggest way.

This woman really didn't like the fact that I was a musician. She didn't like that I used when I was doing my thing and I felt like she was trying to pull me away from music to have some power over me. I was losing my music in exchange for her.

When we separated, my music career resumed at full throttle. I saw how much I had missed playing and I knew music was a must-have in my life. Playing eased the pain of my failed relationship and opened more doors than I could imagine after a few years of relative obscurity. I started a brand-new band that would stretch for over a decade with a revolving cast of characters from my past and some new acquaintances. It was a fruitful and productive time and I still drank too much and was using my usual assortment of chemicals, but I was working up a storm and trying to gain some sort of balance in my life.

By the time the millennium was knocking on our door, I thought I was borderline responsible and dating again. I also spent a generous amount of time visiting and playing in all the local bars. I was living in a rented studio cottage in Mt. Marion, NY and the door was open to all friends and freaks alike. Woodstock '99 happened in Rome, NY, but this time I just enjoyed the party and made some money. Somehow, I didn't dissolve into the ether after that one. It did accelerate the party back home, but, what didn't? In fact, I probably hadn't changed at all.

The most significant and endearing thing to happen to me in 1999 was I met the woman I would spend the next 17 years with. I met her in November 1999, the day before Thanksgiving. I fell hard for her the minute I laid eyes on her and immediately made it a point to get to know her. She was the most beautiful, caring, sexy, intelligent, and creative woman I had ever met.

Since we met, I must say that I have put her through a lot of shit, even right from the start. I was far from the picture of health, but she accepted me for who I was, and I'll never forget that. She's never given up on me when other people have and she's the mother of my two beautiful boys.

I hid a lot of my addiction from her when we first started dating because I was worried that she wouldn't love me, and I didn't want her to see the desperation that came along with being an addict. When we first met, she liked to party a bit and we had a lot of good times doing it, but she was far from entrenched in the addiction angle and could turn it off at will. She is a teacher, an artist, a mother, and just a truly amazing woman. Her tolerance has kept me from doing myself in on more than one occasion.

I was finally happy with my partner, and her family became my own. It was a huge, beautiful, crazy, and loving Italian family. I was right at home and it felt good. When the year ended, I was madly in love and it all felt right. I had even discovered a cure for my alcoholism, albeit in opiate pain medicine. That would soon prove to bring me to my knees, begging for help like never before.

The opiates were cheap and accessible. It seemed like a natural choice for change. Boy was I wrong. I was about to learn some serious life lessons from my exposure and eventual addiction to these substances. In the beginning, they provided all the peace of mind and tranquility I could possibly imagine. At the end, they nearly robbed my soul and took everything precious from me. The infancy of my opiate lifestyle brought forth all the creativity I was looking for from drugs. It was a catalyst for some of the best writing and music I had ever produced up until that point.

I wrote songs like they were falling from the heavens and I was playing live with my band all over the county. I had a new band, terrific girlfriend, and a growing drug addiction. The millennium arrived, the 21st century, I was thirty years old and I had been addicted to one drug or another for 15 years. I didn't manage to compute those numbers back then - I just jumped head first in and never thought twice about any of this being my undoing.

I was going to learn the hard way, the only way I've ever learned. I would take a lot of good people down with me and the valleys and peaks would get deeper and higher as a result. I know now that someone up there in the universe was carrying me.

The Millennium Arrives in the Shape of a Poppy

When 1999 ended, I spent the holidays back at my mom and dad's house. I had a new girlfriend and I really enjoyed becoming close to her and her family. They were, and still are, an awesome bunch of people who never looked down on me because of my wild lifestyle.

The year 2000 brought a lot of change with it — pain medicines were no longer easily available. I hesitantly, but naturally, shifted gears to heroin because it was the only thing that would keep me going in this opiate-haze I was living in. I made pacts with different dealers and did whatever I could to keep the supply coming. I became a drug mule to Newark, NJ and NYC so I could get drugs for free and maintain order in my chaos.

Back then, I just snorted the heroin because I had a fear of needles. I managed to hide my heroin use for just over a year from family and my girlfriend. At least that's what I told myself. But people knew there was something different about me. Even though my alcoholism subsided, I was still a wreck. The only thing that had any normalcy was my relationship and my work. I couldn't even believe I was still able to write and play music, but the creative juices were flowing fast. In those early days of my heroin addiction, it became clear quite suddenly half my day was spent procuring it and thinking about it.

I was arrested in a raid that made the newspaper. My father worked at the local newspaper and he found out immediately. Next, everyone else read it in bold print the following morning. There was no escape - all my family and friends knew. My mother was especially worried, because she thought that I was going to get my girlfriend strung out, too. Thank God that never happened. My girl never indulged, and she didn't approve either. It scared her to see what I had become involved with and was desperate to help me get out from the beginning. It's scary being a heroin addict because you don't know if you're coming or going. All you worry about is that next fix. I can't stress enough how important and utterly strange things are when your addicted to this stuff.

The way you rationalize decisions - the big chances you take - the things you overlook - the chatter in your head — it's all so overwhelming that you can only suppress it by doing more. I was doing everything in my power to maintain a useful existence, but it came with a heavy price tag. It was insanity to the highest degree. At this point in the game I was an alcoholic, cocaine, marijuana, and heroin user and just about as close as you can be to the term "garbage head". I would take any drug as long as it made me feel well and kept my withdrawal at bay.

In late 2000, we moved out of my parent's place and rented an apartment at Skyline Woods in Saugerties, NY. It was a beautiful little place and we both loved it. My memories during this decade tend to get a little scattered because the days melted into months and the months into years. At some point in 2001, I ended up with a felony DWI. My blood alcohol content was 0.17% and I received a sentence of five years' probation.

I knew I was going to have some rough going because I was a heroin addict and on probation you can't drink or use drugs. I kept it hidden as long as I could, but I was petrified about being found out. The seriousness of the issue was knocking me down, I couldn't be in bars anymore, so my music suffered greatly. I had never experienced a consequence like this and I was manipulating the system to stay one step ahead of them, so I could resume my active lifestyle.

I managed to get about a year and some change through it before I violated the terms and conditions. I went to rehab and it kept me clean for about six months, then I went to a community corrections program for three months and got out with an ankle monitor for another sixty days. I violated again in the summer of 2002 and was sent to the Ulster County Jail for my first incarceration. It was horrifying to say the least, and if it wasn't for a Sergeant I knew at the jail, my time would have been even harder to deal with.

I negotiated a six-month sentence after hiring a high-priced lawyer who was also able to vacate the remaining four years. It was the best deal possible; usually you get a full year in jail. When I was released, I had no probation and no one to answer to. I was also temporarily off heroin although I did do it a couple times while I was in jail. I returned home to Skyline and my girlfriend and I were ecstatic to be together again, but it wasn't long before I was back to my old ways smoking crack and sniffing dope. I managed to get back to work and started the band back up again and it was business as usual. I always had a good work ethic instilled by my mom and dad, but a lot of my employers carried me as a liability and burden.

My relationship was deepening, and she made clear she didn't approve of my continuing use. She didn't like the way it was robbing me of my soul and I assured her, as always, that I had my shit under control, even though I knew I didn't. This woman was my greatest ally and I needed her to be on my side, so I would sneak around and try to put on a brave face and not be dope sick around her.

I was living an extremely difficult double life and it wasn't long before she realized that I had a problem that wasn't going away anytime soon. A few months into 2003 I found out I was going to be a father. It hit me with a level of excitement and jolted me with fear. My girlfriend and I decided it would be in my best interest to join the local Methadone Maintenance program, so I could be present for the birth and have a chance to get my affairs in order. It was a quick fix and I stabilized for the first time in many years.

My first son arrived on January 23rd, 2004. It was one of the happiest days of my life. He was born at Northern Dutchess Hospital in Rhinebeck, NY. We were both proud parents and we felt a level of joy like never before. I jumped into being a father with both feet and we moved our new family into a nice little house out in Quarryville, NY between West Saugerties and the Green County line. For a year, it seemed like everything was right and our relationship was really growing. We were financially stable with good jobs and we absolutely adored this little boy that we were blessed with. Both our families were very happy and proud of us and it was a jubilant time.

I had started to develop the urge to do cocaine again after being on Methadone for two years. We held a big party at my house in 2005. All my old drug friends and dealers came out of the woodwork to our humble abode. I snorted coke all day and then smoked crack until dawn. I didn't know this would awaken the sleeping beast and it wasn't long before I was sneaking around smoking crack again. I was still on methadone but now I needed the coke to level me out. I started to drink, and smoke weed as a buffer. I started the downward spiral that I had come to know from previous excursions.

My girlfriend kicked me out after I just flat out refused to stop. I became homeless and really screwed up again. It makes me sad and disillusioned to write these things. It always gets worse, the consequences greater, and it gets harder to stop the momentum when you give it energy. I only sought help when I was so desperate and had nowhere to turn.

From the time my son was born through 2007, I was up and down and in and out of my family unit. Everybody was up in arms over me and they could see a pattern of behavior that they were not able to control. In 2008, I robbed a small store while on a crack binge the day before

Christmas. Two weeks prior, I think I was arrested for possession in Newburgh, NY, too. My life was in shambles and now I was facing more law problems as a result. The new sentence was three years misdemeanor probation out of the Town of Ulster. I immediately violated and went back to jail for another six months. I kicked the Methadone in there and it was one of the hardest detox's I ever went through. I did my time, so I could get back to doing what I did best, fucking up my life.

I went back to heroin as soon as I was released thinking I could keep it together. It didn't work, and I ended up back at the Methadone Clinic for another three years. In-between the heroin run and my subsequent treatment at the clinic I contracted a liver disease from a dirty cotton or spoon. I had started to use needles after about three to four years of just snorting the drug, but we will get into that later.

In the beginning of 2010 my girlfriend became pregnant again. We were living on Yarmouth Street in Kingston, in a small apartment above her sister. I was back to smoking crack and doing my new thing, "scrapping metal," to support my habit. I was doing a lot of petty crimes too and was very lucky to escape some of them.

When we were able to pull our finances together, we moved to Old Lasher Road in Glasco, NY and it afforded us a way to get out of Kingston where the drugs were just blocks away. I was a shell of a person - I had never known who I was, anyway. I was so incapacitated and drifting away that the trouble was brewing on the surface. I was becoming unemployable again and the criminal mentality overtook me. I went to any length to keep my drug intake satisfied.

It's extremely hard looking back like this, if I didn't think it held any therapeutic value, I probably would have never written the first page. When I found out my insurance covered a new drug called Suboxone, another opiate replacement medicine, I switched over from methadone. This gave me the opportunity to not have to go to the clinic every day, and I could get a script once a month from a doctor. I ended up not taking full doses of Suboxone and I sold the rest to raise money to smoke crack. I was fast becoming a casualty again.

2010 was the year of yin-yang. My second son was born October 9th, 2010 at Vassar Hospital in Poughkeepsie, NY. He was a month premature due to my girlfriend having a stressful pregnancy directly correlating to me. I was arrested for possession of stolen property for breaking into a car and stealing credit cards. Both events happened so close to one another that I felt like just jumping off a bridge. My life was in shambles and I couldn't even enjoy the birth of my second son. I was in denial about everything. I was destroying my family with my actions every day. People started to give up on me ever being a solid, caring, and responsible man.

I was facing 1½ to 3 years in State Prison and I just couldn't figure out a way to pull it together. It was the end of the decade and besides the two births of my children I had no idea what I was doing except getting high and going further and further down into the abyss. I would be finding out very soon just how damaged your life can become. I graduated to higher crime, so the consequences weren't going to be slaps on the wrist anymore.

The Needle and the Damage Done

I can't remember exactly when I started using needles, but I do know I snorted heroin for a few years before it came to fruition. I was afraid of needles during my introduction to opiates, but pressure can be a bitch and I eventually caved with the company I kept. One of my neighbors was a drunk, punk, pill head, and one of those people you never forget. At the time of my first injection she was also permanently disabled from the waist down and her habit was through the roof.

One morning, I was over there getting ready to do a few bags and I decided to allow her to do it for me. I just turned my head and let it happen. When the dope hit my blood stream, I felt the familiar rush and I knew I was going to be in trouble. The instantaneous effect of the heroin turned me inside out and now it was going to be administered in an all new way. It was a huge and terrible decision that would have long lasting consequences on my soul.

Each day, for about a month, I would head over to her apartment and ask her to inject me because I couldn't do it myself. Eventually it was too much of a struggle to get myself right and hit her off with some dope too. Financially it was draining me, so I figured it out on my own. At first, I felt like a pin cushion until I managed to do it appropriately. The worst part about injecting drugs is once you cross that line you never go back.

The direct hit is just too damn good. It hits you like a freight train. The euphoria is unexplainable, and you fall in love with the routine as much as you do the drug. When Stephanie found my paraphernalia, she was mortified and totally disgusted. I understood why, but it did nothing to curb my appetite for the drug or how it went into me. I refused to meet anyone even halfway with their demands that I stop or get help. You just keep coming up with these ideas that eventually you will pull it together and everything around you will be alright. It never is, and then years pass by before you even realize that their gone.

I never would look deep into a mirror to see if I was still there or try and see if it was me who was so out of it. Is that the insecure kid who started his journey with beer and pot? Shot full of holes by the needle it's hard to see anything. The man you once were, is no longer evident. You take a leap into something so cunning and powerful it starts to take everything.

Once people know you shoot drugs, you're deemed the lowest of the low on the food chain. It's all gutter trash with infectious diseases and no hope for rehabilitation. You're a stone-cold junkie in the hierarchy of life. The sad part is you don't even care. "Milk blood to keep from running out," Neil Young wrote in his song "The Needle and the Damage Done." It puts the whole thing into perspective. It changes your life. Now, twenty-five years later and thousands upon thousands of shots taken, I sit soul searching in this jail cell.

After five or six years of intravenous drug use, I found out through blood work done at the Methadone Clinic that I was damaging my liver. All I could think was am I going to be alright? How long will I be able to live? Fortunately, it wasn't irreversible damage and I have no permanent damage to my liver.

I find myself unable to forgive myself for what I've done to the people I love, especially my immediate family. The needle and the spoon become the center of my universe. It's the cure all, your lover, your best friend and master. You can't escape its grasp by normal means because its pull is so strong and devious. I know now that's why I'm here in this jail cell writing this book. I tried everything in my power to go get help, but every day I found an excuse to just keep killing myself.

The needle won, I surrendered. It kicked my ass, and I can't go through another battle with it. It brought me places I never would have gone otherwise. It showed me things about myself I would never have done. The sheer power and precision of how it changed my life are unquestionable. There was no other way for me to escape its clutches except to be locked in a cage or found dead somewhere.

I'm really happy to be alive today, I'm even happier that I wake up without poking myself to feel well. You can't put a price tag on being released from its hold, even in a jail cell you can appreciate that your life has been spared and you get another day to fight.

Jails, Prisons, Institutions: Do they Help?

Any junkie knows that the honeymoon is over when you land in county jail. Hell is about to begin. Cold Turkey is in full effect and just the anxiety itself is enough to rattle the walls. You're going to be separated from the one thing that has been killing you, but you need it to survive - you don't want to let it go. It's a double-edged sword, irony to the highest degree.

Knowing you are going to get clean, forced to get clean, is the most horrific thing a junkie goes through. You suck it up and hope you don't end up in a turtle suit on a 48-hour suicide watch. That's how bad it can get and it's terrifying to go through. There is nobody there to tell you it's going to be ok. It's just you and your maker, creator, God, Lord, whatever suits your cries for help.

Does it work? By definition, yes in the short term. Long term? Absolutely not. I have been locked up so much that it was easy for me to believe in a power greater than myself. I begged Him to save me so many times I couldn't even count. When you're a prisoner in any shape or form it's difficult. Mentally, it's so ominous and overwhelming that to getting oriented can take weeks. Any freedom that's compromised is harrowing. It's not just your body that's locked up - you're also a prisoner in your own head.

I've been locked up ten times as an addict and it was never easy. I used to see inmates laughing and carrying on like it didn't bother them. It really freaked me out. I had to learn to do the time and not let the time do me. It didn't come easy for me at all; I had to work at it.

The longest period I was locked up was in 2012 for credit card theft and forgery. I ended up in a "shock" camp - a boot camp of sorts for offenders. You get a military-like heavy duty discipline treatment all day, every day. They concentrate on breaking you down, then building you back up. It was the hardest thing I ever did in my life.

All the while you tell yourself, your family, and anybody that will listen that "this is it", "I'm done", "never again", and you truly mean it. The problem is, addiction is so powerful and insidious you've lost the power to have control over yourself. Maybe addiction can be treated, but you must be so vigilant and involved in recovery, you must put the same amount of work into recovery that you're expending on getting your drug of choice.

When you're locked in these cells and you're alone with your thoughts, you see your life flash like a movie. You see all the wrongs, all the pain, all the craziness. You switch between praying for forgiveness and just going with the flow plotting your next move when your time expires. I've had so many experiences being locked up that I literally felt like I was going insane more than a few times. The detox in jail, especially with opiates, had me howling for relief and begging God for mercy. I was totally drained of my dignity, lying on the floor writhing in agony, and crying out to someone to rescue me.

I have seen some horribly disturbing images in my head while being incarcerated. Things that have made me want to hang up and call it a day. I have seen grown men broken down to nothing with nowhere to turn and no family to help. Right now, after so many of my own arrests and subsequent incarcerations I'm alone, too.

Do I believe these places help? Hell no, but you will get clean. It's a fact – you have no choice. I've always had a tough time being positive because by the time I'm locked up I'm so beaten down. The pleasure centers in my brain are depleted and I'm learning hard lessons. One of them is taking a hard look at yourself. My memories afford me no peace.

The present and the future are my only anchor to life. The past will eat me alive and spit me out. I never thought I would do any time in a jail cell or a rehab. Most of my treatment has been just detox, so I could get in a quick fix and go do it all over again. I never lasted in rehab except two 28-day session, 6 years apart.

As the days pass and I sit here in September 2017 awaiting a 90-day court mandated rehab, I'm grateful that I am still alive and have another chance to make things right by myself and for my family. I'm writing this memoir for healing and to see my own tragic circumstances for what they truly are. I can truthfully tell you I never wanted it to go this far or to be an addict. I want my life back even though I don't even know what it looks like. I've been getting high for so long that it's taken up three quarters of my existence.

At home I have a long-term girlfriend, two beautiful boys, talent, energy, hope, love, creativity, and semi-good health. I have so much to look forward to, but all bets are off if I pick up any drug. I know this. I can't believe I am still alive and not dead from two overdoses and uncountable near-death experiences. I haven't lost my mind completely but rewiring it will take some time for sure.

The real truth, the truth I know, is God is the only one who can save you. It's just my experience. I have a chance to redeem myself. I can recover and stay that way if I work hard at it. Where there's life, there is hope. If there is breath, there is life. I know I've hit rock bottom because it's the only time I have ever admitted defeat and was ready to surrender.

Does my family want me here in jail? I don't know. I do know they consider me safe when I'm locked up and that's a very sad reality to live with. My mom thinks incarceration is the only hope for a junkie, and I understand where she's coming from. She wants me alive - not dead in the gutter somewhere. I remember my mom driving me to a detox/rehab after I just blew $2000 on drugs. I remember her calling me a junkie for the first time. I never liked the term and it hurt me to hear her speak the truth like that.

The question remains, do I think these things help? I really don't know, but I can tell you they are gamechangers. I can't think of anyone wanting to be on the receiving end of such a cold, hard fact. The question remains do these jails, prisons, and institutions help? I don't know, you be the judge.

Family

There have been two men in my life that never turned their back on me or told me I would never be able to get my life right. My father and my girlfriend's dad. They are both deceased now. They were my role models without my even knowing it. These two men always put their family first and worked up until their last days making it happen.

My own father raised me, my brother, and sister. Whenever I was locked up, he would come and see me with support. My girlfriend's dad was a musician and we played together during the last two years of his life. He was down to earth guy who cherished his family. These two men had been through a lot of challenges in their own lives.

Both men had lost their fathers. My dad never really had one to start with. My girlfriend's dad was extremely close to his but lost him to health complications. Both men had very mild experiences with alcohol/drugs as they dealt with the pain of loss from their own life experiences. They both enjoyed a good life, through hard work and strong devotion to their families.

Family is a strange, yet beautiful thing. It can be something to be proud of or something you run away from. I come from a family where addiction and mental health issues were worked out by the individual. None of us wants to admit that the other has a problem and drugs were just another thing you had to work through. I was born into the perfect storm for drug addiction and it became part of my DNA. Drugs were never frowned upon in my family; it was something we accept till this very day.

Sure, when I was a teenager, drugs got me in trouble and I caused some disturbances, but it didn't take long for everyone to just sit back and let my life run its course. I always wished my family stuck together more, even though we have through the most traumatic times. With my dad gone, we all seem to have moved on in our own ways. We've lost our kingpin, our family leader. I looked at my girlfriend's extended family that was so close and so many of them as a godsend. They are your typical Italian family with the gatherings and the big feasts.

I always wanted a family like that. When I met my girlfriend, her family took me in as if I were one of their own and it's been that way ever since. I'd like to say that my own family stood beside me through thick and thin, but as my addiction worsened, they took three steps back. In the end, all I really needed was for them to say "I love you. I understand. You can get it together. I understand what you're going through," and other positive messages. I just don't remember hearing anything like that.

Feeling a sense of abandonment or receiving tough love is a feeling you can't shake off easily. I could never understand the concept of cutting a family member out and then watch them destroy themselves and not at least try to communicate something, anything for that matter. My mother has been a big part of my life, even though she wasn't available much when I was a kid. She has bailed me out of trouble more times than I can count. She provided me with financial stability for most of my life. She also takes on the caregiver role in my place with my children when I'm locked up and incapable of doing my part. Any time I have had a crisis, she has been there for me.

My mom now plays the tough love role and is not affording me the luxury of an easy way out. I believe she loves me, but she also is disgusted with my behavior and how long it's been going on. She is still coping with the extremity of my addiction - the needle didn't help - it freaked her out. When people get wind of you being an IV drug user, they look at you as hardcore, maybe without a chance of recovery. I still think she prays often to help calm her doubts that I will stay clean.

When my mom and dad were going through their ugly divorce, something happened that always stuck in head. Apparently, before I was conceived, my mom had an affair at The Holiday Inn with some guy. My dad found out about it, but they stayed together. When I was finally born, there was a question of my legitimacy as my dad's kid. Turned out, I was his. Later, during the divorce when the fighting was fever pitched my father and older brother use to say that I was her favorite and that I was born at the Holiday Inn. I'll never forget it because I know I shut down and lost faith in a lot of things. I just couldn't believe loved ones could be so cruel.

My parents' divorce was a life altering experience for me. In that moment, I found out about the love and hate that exists between partners. It was a sad day because they were my parents and I loved them both the same. After the divorce the whole dynamic changed, and I would never be the same. The divorce fueled my insecurity and made me feel like I wasn't a true part of the family. I was always being pulled back and forth between my folks, and I was torn between who I wanted to live with.

I forgive and forgot everything and everyone from those early years. Even now, I don't blame anyone or any one instance for me becoming an addict. I still struggle with identifying the reasons why I'm wired this way. I leave it in God's hands now – I find that makes it a bit easier. With my family I never held any grudges, but I still don't understand why our lives were so strained and problematic so very early on in our development.

My sister was the lost child who had a lot of issues growing up. She eventually married and divorced but came away with two beautiful children. She married into the Jewish faith to a guy none of us cared for very much because he looked down on our family. He was not the easiest guy to like and when he decided to leave my sister, we were all relieved.

The only problem is now my sister has very little contact with us and I don't know why, it's just the way it is. It's sad, but I guess it's necessary for her and her own self-preservation.

Holidays used to be important to us as a family but now with my dad gone, we don't even connect over Christmas. My sister endured the family changes and stresses of divorce in a way that I couldn't. I don't know how she processed it. I was able to cloud mine over with drugs, and obviously, it was a temporary fix. She escaped addiction, but she has mental health issues that she continues to work on. I'm always saddened that my relationship with my sister, niece and nephew is non-existent.

My father died of cancer the day before Thanksgiving in 2013. At the time I was six months out of prison and on parole. He was diagnosed with leukemia and we were devastated at how quickly it took him down. I dealt with this loss by getting high again after I'd been clean for a year and a half. It wasn't long before I got locked up again on a violation for transporting heroin across the Mid-Hudson Bridge from Poughkeepsie, NY.

It was bad timing for this horrible event to happen because it really put a huge strain on my dad's health. He was always worried about me and my family and I know it hurt him bad. My father died while I was incarcerated, and I had to attend his funeral in shackles with correction officers in tow. I know my family never forgave me for this.

My mother was the only one who would really speak to me besides my girlfriend and my own children. The word was I accelerated his death by the stress I put on him by being thrown back in jail. I know my father missed me dearly and he wasn't well enough to leave the house or his bed to come and see me like he did in previous incarcerations. It ate me up inside for a long time. I had to believe his soul was with me to just get through the days. My dad, my rock, my main man was gone, and life would never again be the same without his presence.

My family unit crumbled, everyone retreated into their own little lives and all hope and faith in togetherness dissipated. My relationship with my mother is odd at best, because we were always covering for each other's lies in our family.

We are a lot alike whether she admits it or not. We don't like to take responsibility when were wrong. We like to dodge truth and manipulate with perceptions. I guess neither of us wants to admit the part we played in our wrongdoings. We just keep moving and block out the past. I can tell you one thing about my mom and me that are different. She has no problem saying what she feels even if it hurts somebody tremendously. I never got that trait, thank goodness.

My older brother is an alcoholic and an addict in an advanced stage. You would never know it or suspect it unless you were with him late at night after he polishes off an eighteen pack of cheap beer. It's pretty damn scary but he finds a way to maintain. Right now, he lives with my mom and she put up with his alcoholism. She protects him, he's a good boy, he's never robbed her, he's never been incarcerated, and she can trust him. I'm not in that equation because I'm all those things and more.

The people that I believe suffered the most in my family are my girlfriend and my two boys. I can't be a father because of the family court restrictions due to my addiction. I'm on a no contact order of protection modifiable only when they see change. I feel terrible about my overdose and what it did to my family. I carry a guilt from this event and I can only hope and pray that I will redeem myself by recovering from my addiction. Hopefully, the traumatic experience my kids had to witness can be dealt with through therapy. I do resolve to be clean and sober, so I can deal with whatever is next in a healthy manner.

As I close this chapter on family, it's important to point out that I love them with every ounce of my being. I miss them all terribly and, broken or not, they are and always will be my lifeline. I forgive everyone right down the line because I played a part in more than half of the shit that's hit the fan. I know how difficult it is to be a parent. You don't have a guide or map in these territories. I consider myself blessed I have a family.

Being an inmate incarcerated and writing this memoir has opened my eyes to many different feelings. I've been able to see the patterns and parts I have played in my own destruction. Where there is life, there is hope. I have been blessed over and over in my lifetime. I have had chance after chance to change how my life has been played out. I'm lucky to still be alive to tell my story – addiction has killed better people than me. I have been afforded God's grace. I have opportunity. I won't be locked down forever.

Fallout

October 9th, 2010 was the birth of my second son. He came into our lives unexpectedly and seven years after his brother. I would like to say that I went about getting clean and sober for my family, but I was a complete mess. I wasn't using heroin because I was a Suboxone patient, but I was smoking crack, drinking, and committing crimes that would put me in prison for the first time in 2012. I was stealing, lying, and cheating my friends and my family out of anything I could. If it wasn't bolted down, I was taking it and putting it in the trunk of my car.

Crack cocaine is the devil's advocate. It turns decent people into thieves and criminals by default. For the first two years of my son's life, I was nothing but a piece of shit. Looking back, it really bothers me. I've done everything in my power to pray and ask for forgiveness, and it hasn't been easy. The hard part is he's seven years old now and the most adorable and innocent kid you could ever meet. I missed precious years of his development because of my behavior and incarcerations. During this time of being strung out on cocaine, my relationship with Stephanie and my family would end. I got kicked out and became homeless. Until I could clean up, I wasn't wanted or needed in the household.

I would make half-hearted attempts through a detox, but it never stuck. I must have done 25 detox runs, 3 rehabs, and 8 years of opiate replacement therapy. I felt like there was nothing out there that could help me get clean. I started to tell myself I was one of those unfortunate people that they talk about in AA/NA groups. I was constitutionally incapable of grasping any program; my chances were less than slim. I felt like I was born this way and I would carry on to the bitter end.

Jeffrey Bovee

I committed a crime involving stolen credit cards in 2012 and was sentenced to 1½ - 3 years in state prison. They offered me drug court, but when the van came to take me to an 8-month rehab, I backed out and elected to do my time. I ended up in Lakeview Correctional Facility in Brocton, NY on Lake Erie in Western NY.

Brocton was a shock facility where they incorporated military-style discipline with drug treatment and work details. I went through the whole reception experience in the New York State Corrections from Downstate to Ulster and then up to Lakeview on a ten-hour bus ride shackled to another man. I was issued the state greens and stripped down naked. They put me under the cold shower and gave me this shit to get any bugs off my body. They push you through all the classification stuff like a herd of cattle. It was demoralizing to say the least, but I got through it.

My dad came to visit me before he realized he was sick, like clockwork he was there for me. I always remember my dad being there for me. Even though we had our issues with one another, he was my rock. My dad dealt with my shortcomings in a way that was completely different then my how my mom did. He took loving care of my family and I, and he loved my children very much. He was a great man, I could only dream to be like him.

I spent a year up in the prison boot camp and returned home on parole in May 2013. I was 43 years old and in the worst shape of my life. Brocton was the hardest time I ever did. It was one of those eye-opening experiences. It was valuable, and I don't regret doing it, but I do regret putting my family through the shit I was going through.

The problem was, I didn't use the tools I learned and, six months into my parole, I violated the terms and conditions by getting arrested transporting heroin. I had been doing the downtown trips to my dealer for prescription meds and it wasn't long before I picked up on the dope again. I was shooting oxycodone, dilaudid, and morphine pills along with heroin. I used my dad's cancer diagnosis as reason for my relapse, but the real fact was I just wanted to get high again. It's what I know best. I was beyond depressed and it sent me further down into the gutter.

The following day I was back in custody and heading to prison again. I received a 90-day violation sentence at Willard Drug Treatment campus. It's just another form of "shock" but shorter. My father died when I was in custody, and I was destroyed by it. I did my time and returned to Woodstock to see my girlfriend and kids. I was on parole again and started an outpatient drug program and went back on Suboxone, so I wouldn't be tempted to do opiates. Surprisingly my life started to get better. I kept myself in decent shape and remained clean; I was doing well for a change.

I found work that I loved with a previous employer and my relationships with everyone stabilized. When I was near my last week of parole I went downtown and ordered up a cocktail of prescription opiates that I proceeded to shoot into my veins. I fell right back into my old ways and I started my downward spiral all over again. I was back to playing music in a new band and everyone picked up on the attitudes and behaviors that surround a junkie. The drugs just rob you of everything that is sacred in life. You lose everything over and over and it still doesn't change a goddamn thing. The only way out is surrender and admitting defeat. You put it off, till you're left with nothing.

By 2016 I was a full-blown junkie again, and I sold my replacement meds for dope. I was running hard and trying to feed this monster habit I developed. I couldn't take care of myself let alone my family and every dollar made went to the dope man. I was right back into a meaningless existence, and my family was suffering right there with me. We couldn't get along because none of them approved of my addiction. My entire world was centered on what was in the spoon.

I overdosed for the first time in my life on September 26th, 2015 at my home in Woodstock. It happened again on March 29th, 2017. Both overdoses involved Child protective Services. The second time it happened, I was ordered into Family Court with Orders of Protection all around. I was removed from my household and charged criminally with Endangering the Welfare of a Child. When I went home to get some of my property, I was also charged with criminal contempt for violating the orders in place resulting in a four-week sentence. I was jailed a second time for petit larceny when I stole two bicycles from a Target store to feed my heroin addiction.

In Orange County, the judge was really rough on me. The initial sentence was for six months, but I ended up sitting in the Orange County Jail for a month and then opted out for a 90-day rehab program at St. Christopher's Inn in Garrison, NY. I've never been to the place, but I heard it was the best place to get clean in the state.

While here in jail I haven't communicated with anyone on the outside of these walls. It's been a real wake up call for me. I finally surrendered and admitted losing the battle. This war is over. I can't fight anymore. I've lost everything, including my will to live in active addiction. I was trying to kill myself. I know that now. I reached out in desperation to God and he somehow pulled me out of the gutter and set me on a path to healing. God always saves us sinners, if you let him. That's a fact for me.

Where Do I Go from Here?

Where do I go from here? This question eludes me every day. Right now, it's September 8th, 2017 and I'm cooling my heels in the Orange County jail 50 miles from my home. Sometimes it's surreal, how I got here. I'm an addict behind bars and it's an eye-opening experience. I'm learning to sink or swim quickly. I pray daily, I read and write, I try to get my strength back, and when I feel talkative, I look for a fellow inmate. I don't glorify any of my drug use. I do the very best I can with the circumstances that I was dealt with from the judge. I'm thinking that I am one of the lucky ones because I'm alive and I am going for further treatment.

When I arrived here, and the drugs were still coursing through my system I wanted to die and tried hanging myself in my cell. Thank God there's nothing to hang from, otherwise I'd be gone for sure. Today I want to live, and I feel like I have a fighting chance. In my mind there's a lot of soul searching happening. I stick to a routine to feel human. I need a sense of normalcy and to not feel like a caged animal. It's all on God's time behind these walls. I don't know anything more than my next step is long term rehab at a place called St. Christopher's. I'm really looking forward to getting out of this jumpsuit and putting my feet on the ground. Never in my life have I wanted drug treatment so badly.

I'm so beat down that I'm sure there's a better way for me. It's one of the only times I really reached out for help. I signed on to treatment and I'm not even stressing it being 90 days. In the past, even though I've been incarcerated longer than that, I looked at that kind of time in a

Jeffrey Bovee

rehab as a death sentence. I just keep praying that this obsession for drugs will leave me and I can someday resume some sort of life outside of an institution.

I feel the need to be more spiritual and St. Christopher's could give that to me. I need to be somewhere that can help me get in tune with myself. I have been living so selfishly that I don't even know where I fit in the great scheme of things. I have spent decades destroying myself and I don't know where to go anymore. I need to get better for myself and my family. I'm way overdue. I'm tired of being a prisoner, and I don't want to die and leave my family behind.

Writing these pages has helped me look hard at all the questions I could never answer. My family is gone while I'm here in this cell. There is nobody to call, nobody to answer the endless streams of letters I send. I'm currently in a holding pattern, kind of like a plane circling a storm waiting for the best possible clearing to land. The stormy weather of the past 35 years filled with every substance available to man.

It clogged up my brain, and it really did drive me insane. Thank God those things are starting to clear up for me now. There's a greater plan for me. I have become a new project. Will there be stormy weather? Of course, Will there be detractors? Without a doubt, nobody trusts a junkie. The only peace I find is in my higher power. He is on my side. I owe myself and my family a better life. There's no real fun in being an addict at the end of a 35-year run. In the beginning, the consequences were superficial and distant. In mid-life, those same consequences feel much more real and close, as if they can now dismantle my entire life.

God's Gifts

My love for music became apparent when I was four years old. I used to listen to 45s and LPs with my family religiously. The 70s were a wonderful time to get turned on to music. Between my older brother and my parents, I was bombarded with everything from soul to rock n roll. I was a rock n roller from the beginning. It was in my DNA, coursing through my veins, beating in my heart and soul.

By the time I was 10-11 years old, I knew more about the history of rock than some DJ's on classic rock radio. I loved the Rolling Stones, the Beatles, the Grateful Dead, Bob Dylan, Pink Floyd, and the Doors. They were the soundtrack to my upbringing, my daily bread. I lived and breathed music. I knew every song, every album, and every lyric of my favorite bands. When I realized I could start playing the songs of my heroes, I picked up the keyboard and guitar.

I started playing in a band in 1986 when I was sixteen years old. It's been my calling ever since. It's a God-given gift that can't be ignored. Music gives me a tremendous amount of joy and freedom. I love to entertain people and see them having a good time, breaking free from the daily grind. I started writing songs when I was thirteen years old and since then I've created a hundred songs, and even more poems, stories, and observations. When I was younger, I couldn't turn the inspiration off it flowed so freely. Music and writing for me was the most natural fit I ever encountered.

It's all I ever wanted to do. I realize now how intricately the alcohol and drugs played a part in it. Addiction took away my ability to focus on what really mattered. I couldn't immerse myself in music and writing sufficiently to make a living at it. I'm not saying music didn't put money in my pocket, but the kind of success I wanted to attain eluded me. Addiction becomes a second full-time job in procuring and using them.

Music saved me so many times as a young man. It helped redirect my energy and lubricate my insecurity. I have spent more than half my life playing music and writing with varying degrees of success. I've made thousands of people happy and reached as many or more through writing. It really is a gift from God. There's no other explanation. I try to tell myself as I sit here in my jail cell, locked away from my precious freedom, that my plight is temporary. I'm lucky that I can read and write. Writing is my salvation and gives me a purpose to continue. It forces me to look at myself critically and understand the patterns of abuse. I'll always have my music and I will get back to it again. If I can clean up my side of the street, I'll afford myself more days to play and write.

My track record with the musicians in the Hudson Valley is sketchy at best right now. An addict is a liability to any band and that's how everyone knows me. I admit that some of my most pivotal creative bursts have been fueled by narcotics. Fear and insecurity are killers of creativity. Being high removes your self-doubt and allows everything to flow more easily. I'm going to have to overcome fear and insecurity to do this without drugs. The simple fact of being able to convey feelings through music and writing is priceless. Like freedom, you just can't put a price tag on it. Creativity flows like an energy field. If you can direct the message, the people will receive it.

Each day that goes by without me getting high is a step in the right direction. Writing often is slowly developing more spontaneity and the pages are easier to fill. I feel blessed that I've made it this far. It's been a steep learning curve. All the receptors in my brain have been affected and need to heal. Every day is a struggle and a blessing.

Writing this book and opening channels has helped me more than could ever describe. My life is laid out before me in black and white text.

It makes me cringe to admit my wrong doings, but it's a healthy task I must undertake, nonetheless. Being incarcerated is saving me. I'm starting to find ways to communicate my feelings in a healthy manner. Missing this opportunity would be a real bummer - I'm not even going to pretend.

Looking back on hundreds of shows with multiple bands with varying degrees of success and styles is comforting. I have had the honor of playing with a rotating cast of musicians. The gratification of playing with such talented musicians has been exciting and rewarding. I'm not going to sugarcoat the fact that alcohol and drugs fueled a lot of performance and sessions because it did. Social and creative lubricants like marijuana seem like mainstays in the musical community.

Every musician has a sense of adventure and wants to play without a net – to be improvisational and spontaneous. There's a great struggle as performers in our own right. We put up a lot of walls to keep our creativity close to us, the universal mind. When you write, draw, paint, play an instrument, it is a gift from above. When you fail to put these creations it into motion and disregard them, you become off balance. I don't take any of this for granted. Life deals us a lot of blows, addict or not. You must find a way to live, create, and be of service in some sensible and healthy way, and still be able to harness all kinds of unsuitable energies and challenges that make art the coolest thing on the planet!

My music career is on a temporary hiatus. I can accept this. I know rebuilding takes time, and I'm in no rush. I have so many personal matters that need attention that it might be quite a while before I can return to the stage. When I do return, I want it to show my best.

The Present and the Future

Today has been a rough day. It's Saturday September 10th, 2017 and I am exactly where I'm supposed to be in the eyes of the state of New York, in a jail cell. I keep telling myself that God has a plan for me. It involves rejuvenation - a plan to wash me clean. The hardest thing I've had to learn living in the present moment is acceptance. That no matter what, if there is something or someone bothering me it's related to the fact I'm resisting.

Life has dealt me some heavy blows and I've had a hand in all of them. I have been trying to utilize this experience as a time for reflection and healing. I would be lying to you if I said I wasn't depressed, but there is another side. It is a hopeful one I had to dredge out of the pit of my soul. Before I was arrested, I was losing faith and hope in everything. I just wanted the pain and despair to end. All I could do was use drugs to kill the pain; it was the only way I knew.

I knew upon arrival to incarceration that I was going to face my demons head on. The isolation forces me to sit here and dwell inside my head. It's bound to get a little problematic. I'm going to be alright, I keep telling myself, like a mantra. I would be dead otherwise; it just is that kind of detox. Every problem has a solution it's the law of the universe. It's an escape hatch that I'm very aware of, especially in tough times.

If there wasn't a specific reason for me to be alive today, I wouldn't be here today. I had to grow spiritual wings as soon as my freedom was compromised. It happens all too naturally when the shit hits the fan. When I was on the street, I prayed just to get what I needed and relieve me of the pain. Sometimes, I prayed for Him to just take my life because all I did was hurt everyone. I couldn't, for the life of me, stop the insanity I was going through. The addiction was going to check me out permanently, but I always woke up and started the process all over again. It was evident that something far worse than incarceration was going to happen.

The cloud of despair was above me every morning when I awoke in the strange, filthy, cockroach-ridden house I was living in before my arrest. I lived in Newburgh, NY for one reason and one reason only. Cheap and available drugs! If I had stayed in Woodstock, I would have been locked up much sooner and for a much longer period. I stuck out like a sore thumb on my rural streets back home. Here in Newburgh, I'm like the rest of the Walking Dead. We number in the hundreds.

I am trying to remind myself this jail cell is temporary. I'm doing a lot of soul searching, I'm trying to love myself. It's essential I get my head on right. The present is the past as soon as I'm done with a sentence. My dreams are all in the future and it keeps me going. God makes dreams one size too big, so we can grow into them.

To quote Zig Ziglar, "There are no traffic jams on the extra mile" - I must understand that this is just a small chunk of time. At the very least, I'm getting stronger, better, and faster. What does the future hold for Jeffrey Michael Bovee? The changes are coming, and they are abundant. I am super aware that I have a considerable bunch of hoops to jump through. I never give myself a chance; I never take ownership for my actions until it's too late. Life is beautiful, life is painful, and life is life on life's terms. One day you're on top, the next you're in the gutter. It's how I react to change that makes or breaks every bleak situation.

I don't know anything about the future beyond today. I could die tonight in my sleep and someone else would take my writings and toss them away. You just don't ever know. This writing has been gratifying; I knew I had it in me. I have a good feeling about this story helping other people. We are one. You are not alone. The pain, the endless chatter, is in our head, and it is temporary. The addiction and abuse can be resolved. You have to believe.

How an addiction will end is the question. Hopefully, any addict reading this book will end their addiction as I plan to: with a future. Maybe you won't have to go the extremes that I did. I sure the hell hope not, because you need an unwavering constitution for pain. I wouldn't wish my addiction and the problems it's caused on my worst enemy. The paradox is, I think my past has made me a better person as a result of the information and introspection I've gathered over this long journey. Today, as painful as my situation is, the words are just flowing off my pen. I just clocked forty-five minutes of continuous writing and, as a lefty, that's no easy feat.

I'm amazed by how much ink I've gone through. And, me being amazed doesn't happen often in this life. The pen I'm using is considered contraband because it's a regular one. They figure you can stab somebody with it. I have to navigate the rounds of the corrections officers and their cell searches, so I can do my thing and not catch an extra charge. I get their flimsy little pens and take the ink tube out and load it into the good one and it's a wrap. The pen was in this cell when they moved me here on this unit. Call it what you will, I call it divine intervention! I wouldn't have been able to write this story any other way.

I'm learning hard, but valuable lessons. Is it different learning these truths in a jail cell? Most certainly. The difference is that I'm alive and I have the opportunity to start all over again. Opportunities don't always exist for addicts. Usually, these opportunities have all been ignored and left unused and undiscovered. God has always been extra kind to me. He has worked overtime on me. He has never left my side, even in the most destitute and problematic times. I feel bad that I didn't honor my life or His role in supporting me.

Who am I?

Who am I? I can't remember exactly when or where I was asked this question, but I'm guessing it was during one of my failed attempts trying to get clean. Mind you, I say clean, I really should say detoxed. I have been afraid to do more than 3-5 days at a clip because I just had to get back to getting high, usually in a different and more successful way. I never do get clean and I end up just chasing another episode that ends up with me in ruins.

Today, I am locked up tight in cellblock C2 cell 38. It's been my home since August 17th, 2017. The date as I write this is September 9th, 2017. I went through my forced detox and I'm slowly coming back to life, one brain cell at a time, 24 hours a day, 3 meals a day. I go to sleep at 9pm and get up at 6am. My day begins and ends in prayer. It's been a difficult journey. It's never an easy task when you're locked down.

You need to keep your head up and look forward to the prize. Awareness is the key and today I am more than just a junkie on the streets. I know that God is out there pulling for me to get better. I knew that as an active user, too, but something is changing. Who am I? I'm a writer, observer, adventurer, father, son, boyfriend, and student. I have more to look forward to then I did 3½ weeks ago when I was pan-handling 3 times a day to just get high. That was a meaningless existence. I had put all my energy into getting high and staying that way. Now, I owe it to myself and my family to try something new and completely out of my comfort zone.

Who am I? I am an addict looking to recover and manage my own life. When you're an addict and you to start to get clean, all sorts of mental things start coming back into play. The mere fact that you have been checking out all day, every day, for years is very significant when it comes to the balancing act of healing your mind, body, and spirit. It's fascinating stuff, the stasis that is at stake. For my whole life, I couldn't imagine not using drugs in one form or another. One day, something happens, and you decide to get off the merry-go-round.

You admit defeat. The war is over. I surrender, I'm beat, and the game is over. The best feeling, I know now, is not waging a war to stay high every day. I also know the flip side of the difficult work needed to stay clean. But I know I'm worth it today. I am strong, intelligent, kind, compassionate, and hopeful. I am much more than I give myself credit for. I am a human being with defects, I am a friend, I am the one person who never thought he would make it.

Revisiting the Grateful Dead Experience

I may be going to hell in a bucket, baby, but at least I'm enjoying the ride! It was 1985-1995 and I was enjoying 10 years on the road with the Grateful Dead. It was an amazing journey with friends who have come and gone. The Dead were a band that just literally smoked on a hot night and took us across the USA looking for good times in high places. The Grateful Dead is, and will always be, my favorite band of all time. Maybe it was all the biblical references in their songs. Maybe it was the outcasts, gamblers, travelers, and circus freaks. I believe it was a little of everything. It was just surreal that it even happened.

I know one thing; no band has ever rocked out in such an open and free form way before or since the last note was played. The Grateful Dead was a culture of likeminded people seeking adventure in the American landscape and the cosmos. We were road people cruising the highways and byways, the arteries of every city. We enjoyed the psychedelic experience above and beyond the normal human capacity. We were like Jesus' ministry in the beginning, we cared for one another and the music was the healing power, our holy grail. The music enveloped your soul and still does every time I listen to it today.

The whole Dead package delivered so much and in so many gratifying ways, it was one of a kind. It could be country, rock n roll, blues, jazz, acid rock, and folk all in the same night. The lyrics written by Robert Hunter and John Barlow were literary works of art. They were archaic tales that always had a great storyline. Whether it was the soulful delivery of Jerry or the over-the-top rock of Bob Weir, it was the greatest show on earth. The light shows were intense and psychedelic, and the sound system was crystal clear even in stadiums with 80,000 fans. Every detail was paid close attention to for the deadheads, right down to camping accommodations.

Grateful Dead music is deep, poetic stuff and it transports you. The music takes you on a journey into the frontier and deep space, just awesome memories looking back. I was blessed to see a hundred shows all over America, it's something special and I'll never forget those days. But, not without problems, the scene grew quickly, and problems started cropping up with ticketless hordes and harder drugs. I was able to get an amazing 10 year run out of it. I was grateful indeed, no pun intended.

The consequences of getting high back then were beyond the horizon. I was 15 at my first show and 25 when the long strange trip ended. When Jerry Garcia died in 1995, the whole bus came to an abrupt halt. I'll never forget the day I got the call from my friend. I was at my mom's house smoking crack by myself on a summer afternoon. Jerry's death didn't really hit me until the next day because I was so high, I couldn't process anything.

Jerry was a junkie too, but he was seeking treatment. His body was so polluted, he died of a heart attack in his sleep while withdrawing. He was really trying to clean his act up and sometimes I wonder what life would have been like if he was still alive. It was a sad day in music history and the whole scene changed as a result. The grateful dead experience was all about freedom. You could be as strange or square as you wanted, and no one cared.

The Grateful Dead is a huge part of who I am and will always be close to my heart and spirit. I still wish the bus was rolling down the highway and wonder what it would be like now. I wish I was a headlight on a northbound train. I never attended a show sober. There was always a cocktail of mind-altering substances. My life wouldn't be the same if I wasn't part of the scene. I have a fondness for the band and my fellow Deadheads and I get excited when I meet others who shared the same trip. We are everywhere as the old bumper sticker proclaimed.

After Jerry died, the band came around in different configurations and it was wonderful too, just a bit different. I did have fun and I always went to pay homage to the remaining members. The best part of their continuing was being able to share it with my girlfriend. She never saw the band with Jerry in it but got a taste of the community, nonetheless. I love that the Dead keep rolling along; they play for the love and magic, for the community. It really is true that the music never stopped. I think it's fitting to close with the opening lyrics from Stella Blue, written by Robert Hunter. "All the years combine, they melt into a dream."

Hope

You have to believe, you have to have faith, you have to be strong, and you have to give yourself a chance. This is my mantra today and every day! Lord God, Heavenly Father, make me whole again. Let me be an instrument of your Peace. It's comfort from above that gives undeniable freedom. You have to know there is a sincere endeavor from the Holy Spirit. I have always been a believer in a higher power; I choose to call him God. He has saved me so many times in and out of my addiction.

I have done so many horrible things to myself and others. Half of them I wasn't punished for. If I had been caught, I would be in state prison doing hard time. There is a thing called hope, a belief that things can and will get better, or at least change. That all the pain and uncertainty isn't in vain. That there is a bigger plan for the man! Every day, I thank God that he spared my life and gave me breath. I don't take it for granted when I'm clean. My obstacle is remembering the misery of addiction and keeping it front and center. Hope is my new survival tool every living moment.

When you're locked down like this, nobody has a kind word or gesture. No one cares about your situation. When I tell an inmate that I'm going to drug treatment, they say "Just do your time." This isn't the place for positive change. If you listen to the chatter it can really bring you down and put you on edge. Hope reminds me this is temporary. The clock will forge on - I'm not going to be here forever.

I'm an addict. I have a lot of healing work ahead of me. I hate saying I have a disease, but I can't reasonably explain why I would do the things

Jeffrey Bovee

I do unless it really were true. Hope is everything in these troubled times. I know I am going to be alright when I'm hopeful and faithful. I am interested in treatment because I know already this institution is going to spit me back out on to the streets. It speaks volumes about the disconnection from society. I'm looking at my freedom as going to rehab, it's a no brainer. There is hope in the messages I receive from above, if I can quiet my mind enough. With each day that passes me by, I am one step closer to my eventual freedom. I hope this obsession leaves me for good, once and for all. I'm no fool though, I'm incarcerated and it's much harder on the outside. There is no sense in pretending that this is going to be an easy trek. Addiction is a relentless beast, a monster always waiting to be fed and awakened. I make no mistake in seeing it any other way. It's a force of darkness and destruction. It doesn't care about anything but your demise and the company of your banishment.

I sit and wonder why sometimes why I could never accept the consequences for what they were. I kept running through the giant stop sign, the warning lights, missing the real signs of wisdom. I still can't for the life of me explain why I let it take me down so far, it just did. By all accounts, I had nothing left to lose, except my life. Really, I just wanted it to be over and it's awful saying that. I do have a soul and the ability to get better. Getting clean and sober is the only way I can go on. It's the only way out. If not, it's just more of the same thing I'm trying to avoid, pain...

Resentments

Resentments surround me like mosquitos. I know it's wrong for me to keep them around, especially resentments towards the people who love me most. I need to forgive myself and my loved ones because I got locked up because of my choices and decisions. It's hard though, to not be angry about certain events that seem to have contributed to my addiction. In some ways, I feel betrayed in my addict's mind.

I harbor resentment to my family, because I'm locked up and they won't communicate with me. My biggest resentment is towards my mom, the person that is closest to me. All my life, she has been there when I've beaten myself to the ground. She always helped pick up the pieces. She tried her best to deflect the negative from my life. Then one day, she just stopped doing it. I feel like I should blame her shrink, who feeds her the tough love piece. Right now, she's gone; she's not going to rescue me or the addict in me. The truth hurts and fuels my resentment.

I say to myself if it was my kid were following my addiction, I would never turn my back on him. It feels like being abandoned, something I have always had a problem with in my life. My folks did the best they could but there were so many variables growing up I could never see straight. Alcohol and drugs were comfortable. I was sent mixed messages as a kid and I had no supervision. We all got high together at one time or another; I know we shared a drink or two.

I feel like I didn't know the truth about where drugs were going to lead me, and I always had trouble asking for help. My parents were busy living their lives and I was left to my own devices. My mother has two sides, a super-caring and kind one and a crafty, rude one. You never know

Jeffrey Bovee

which side you'll be on and you'd better pray she doesn't cut you off, because it's harsh and certain when she does.

Since my father died, my mother has put on a tougher skin. You have to peel back the layers to reveal her compassionate side. I know she is tired of rescuing her adult children. She is tired of bullshit and everything I put this family through. I know she won't completely blot me out of the sky, but she is clearly making me sweat it out. When she gets an inkling that I'm using drugs she turns off her emotions and that bothers me because I need to communicate my pain to her. It's true not everyone is sympathetic, especially with junkies.

I resent addiction. I have children of my own and I'm ruining their lives through my actions. This addiction is the monster; I wish I never fed the damn thing. I was a kid when I started, 11 years old for Christ's sake. I had no idea what the hell was happening until it was way too late, and that is the truth. Drugs start innocently and secretively and then sneak up on you and trap you in their web. It's all warm and fuzzy in the beginning and then angular and obtuse in the end.

The good news I can be treated, and I can have a wonderful life. My family has been waiting decades for me to transpire. All the jails, institutions, and near-death episodes leave people wondering where it will end. I'm sure more than a few are saying to the bitter end.

I feel despair because there's nothing left sometimes. All the love is gone and I'm going to be alone forever. My mind plays tricks on me because I will always have a higher power. When you're an addict, it's tragedy after tragedy. When I'm clean, life is good, it just doesn't last long before the wheels fall off again. I know deep inside my resentments are shallow attempts to hold someone responsible besides myself. It keeps me sick. It keeps me groveling in the dirt.

I just have this thing in my head that keeps me from remembering all the pain; call it a built-in forgetter. I don't know man, this is some slippery territory. One day, I hope and pray to be relieved off this madness. I deserve a better life than what I've lived and what I'm giving my family. The mechanics of addiction are very insidious. I need to remember not to complicate this recovery business. I'm learning but I'm never too far from allowing it to start all over again.

When I think about it now, maybe my biggest resentment is against myself. I let myself down and did nothing about it, all I had to do was ask for help. Wow! Could it be that simple? I really don't have a clue...

Finding my Vein of Gold

Incarceration can unravel your senses. It can break you down in many ways. It's psychologically trying, because you go through so many different emotions. If you're an addict like me cleaning up it's like a roller coaster ride. The first two weeks are consumed detoxing and getting my head right. It wreaks havoc on my senses - the neural pathways are in crisis mode. The stranger in a strange land syndrome is omnipresent. I'm fighting a war to just feel normal again. It's tricky stuff when you have to swim upstream or sink. You have to give yourself a chance to recuperate.

My life has been a series of extreme highs and abysmal lows. As a creative person I try to see the vein of gold in all the pain and suffering. You have to find a way to allow yourself to feel again and that can be terrifying without the drugs you're so use to ingesting to kill all the pain. These psychic wars are debilitating, and the sleepless nights seem never ending. Sometimes you want to give up because you're so beat down and a shell of your true self.

I just finished a letter here in my cell to my mother. It kicked up some heavy shit. The emotions are fragmented and fleeting. I'm starting to feel again, the good and the bad, it feels right somehow, the emotional vulnerability mining the vein of gold. The place where you know your calling in life, a life changing event unfolding. I admit that prayer has helped more than anything and it has become constant in my day.

There are a lot of addicts and inmates that feel pain and turn to God. It's nothing to be ashamed about. In fact, it's a sure way to redemption. I have fought tooth and nail with my demons to get my head on straight. God hasn't forsaken me, and he lifted my spirit up, that's a fact. When I speak of these things, I'm no holy roller, I'm merely exuding the truth. I've been down so goddamn long that it looks like up to me, like an old blues refrain. I want to know what it's like to be a human being and not a toxic dumping ground for alcohol and drugs. When I tell you that I don't know what it's like, believe me and lift me up, I need more help than you could imagine.

There was a time in my life in 1999-2000, the holiday season when my sister bought me a book for Christmas to help me out and let go of the pain. It was called "The Vein of Gold," by Julia Cameron. Although, I didn't follow it precisely (it doesn't condone drug use!) I did manage to explore and heal from the exercises and teachings. I actually pulled myself out of the pain I was experiencing at that time. Learning to be kind to myself was something completely new to me. The book opened doors that were closed before and it fed my creativity. It helped me to exercise my creativity, it lit the spark again.

The prayer walks, artist dates, the nurturing aspects of menial life tasks, that book was just what the doctor ordered, but not enough to stop me from becoming engulfed in the womb of opiate addiction. Unfortunately, they segued quite naturally into one another. I certainly knew I was on a road less traveled. There is a reason why there's less traffic sometimes. After trouble started to infiltrate, I started to learn the hard way. I wish I would have heeded the call.

I don't like to think people are smarter or more aware, but addiction doesn't touch everyone. I'm happy that's the case, because I sense it could be a much larger crisis and epidemic then it is. The one thing I want to stress as I awaken here in my jail cell on another beautiful August day is "there are lessons to be learned here." My learnings in patience and the healing is what keeps me going. The drugs are leaving my mind and body and it's a wonderful feeling to wake up and not have to stick a needle in my arm to live another day.

I always used to get trapped in the "why me?" mentality. I don't want to be here locked in a cage, but here I am, and I better make this situation work for me. I was so close to death and I ignored every sign. I hope that I have finally seen the grace and blessing in rescuing me from myself. Is it a hard piece to chew, without a doubt brother! The Vein of Gold that runs through everything...

Higher Power

Living life as an addict creates a spiritual dysfunction. All hope is tied to next hit. In the beginning, getting high is comfortable and cool. Then it just turns you inside out. You begin to cocoon and isolate yourself, then addition takes everything sacred and precious in your life away from you. Addicts lose sight of the need for respecting a higher power. It doesn't matter who or what it is that brings you the strength and solitude. What does matter is that we are alive and that we believe there is something greater than us.

We all feel it – a conscience, the little voice in the back of your head, the gut feeling – there is something in this world that is beyond our explanation that is always helping to guide us. Sometimes, we listen. Many times, though, we ignore this support and pass it off as our own twisted mind trying to trick us. Once you stop believing, it's hard to see the silver lining in anything.

My addiction has spanned decades, so I had to be aware that it might take a miracle to save someone like me. I choose to call my higher power God, Lord, Jesus Christ, and Holy Spirit. I'm not trying to convert anyone or say this is the only way, but it's what came to me. I recognize that He has saved my ass so many times it's scary. There have been the arrests that never came, the resuscitations from overdoses, accidents that could have be much worse, and relationships that were saved.

As you know, I've done a lot of drugs for a very long time. In the darkest hour, when I've cried out for help, my higher power has always been there. He was waiting for me to ask. The foxhole prayers of "I'll never do this again, please save me" were endless. There have been hundreds of times when He watched over me and spared me of even harder time in jails and institutions. I never got caught for probably half of the crimes that I've committed. The crimes against my family and society at large have been vacated but not forgotten.

To be an addict there is no other way but to lie, cheat, and steal. When I was active and running around every day, He held me close and waited patiently planning an upwards path. I never walked alone out there - it was God's grace that saved me from an ultimate death. But I've learned that you must be open to listen to God's help. You need to reach out to God, or your higher power, and admit your powerlessness, accept defeat, and surrender. Only then will you see true salvation.

Your higher power becomes your one and only lifeline. This spiritual energy will repair you. There's no time table so patience, hope, and faith are imperative. I've missed so many things because I wasn't listening. But He has allowed me to cherish even the simplest things like sunsets, a soft rain, the clean world after a fresh snowfall, the changing seasons, and the journey from pain to promise. He blessed me with a family.

I'm here to tell you that you don't have to kill yourself anymore. The pain does stop, even in a jail cell. With faith comes hope and addiction can stop. I was saved from the brink of total self-destruction.

Can I get a Hallelujah?!

Bridging the Present and the Future

Today, I will be released on my own recognizance to the Orange County Probation department for treatment at St. Christopher's Drug and Alcohol Program. I'm finally leaving this facility - I do want to get out of here! Treatment centers are always overcrowded with long waiting lists, so hopefully, I won't be sitting here for weeks on end. I have to kick my addiction – this is life or death for me and there are hundreds or thousands of people waiting to get into these treatment centers.

A treatment center offers relief to the sick and suffering who voluntarily sign in, and they are also holding pens for mandated offenders like me who are afforded second and third chances at possibly getting it right. It's a time out for some, a time for regeneration and removal from their current affliction and environment. These centers can also serve as homeless shelters for addicts that ran out of time and money and are about to enter the circle of jails, institutions or death.

Recovery is a big business these days with the opiate epidemic reaching astronomical proportions. It's sad in a way because a lot of addicts won't get the help they need. They will get high again and start the cycle all over. I've been there. The reality is all we have is today. Tomorrow is not a promise or guarantee. We certainly expect it to be there when the sun rises, but it you never know the kind of hand that will be dealt to you. The odds are against us is what I'm trying to say. I go to sleep each night and thank God for giving me this life, no matter how destitute or broken my spirit is.

95

I have been praying since I was a young man, both while addicted and recovering. My connection with God runs deep; he has carried me throughout my journey. The present situation is right in my face. I'm an inmate at the Orange County Jail facing two counts of misdemeanor petit larceny, the maximum sentence being 1-2 years' incarceration. I'm going to end up doing 30 days locked down and then 90 days of treatment to hopefully vacate or lower the charges.

Right now, I'm waiting to be transported on September 19th, 2017 to rehab. It will be my first rehab in 17 years and my first long term treatment ever. I'm 46 years old and I have been using since I was 11 years old. I've only not used for a total of two years due to previous incarcerations. The sheer weight of that statement really gets under my skin. The 36 years of getting high on either alcohol, pot, psychedelics, cocaine, opiates and whatever else was available has worn me out and dragged me down. I know I have a very hard journey ahead of me and I can't falter.

I do a lot of thinking and daydreaming about my current situation. I beat myself up over the horrible things I've done to people that I love and to society at large. So many people have wiped their hands clean of me or just plain given up on the hope that I could possibly change. Most of my friends and family have said "I've had enough" or "to hell with you." This story is the only testimonial to how my life unraveled and it is a fair representation of my problem. The day I started this book, the sheer magnitude of the task at hand was overwhelming. Each day, I try to fill up a page and it is exhausting on the mind. When I get to the point that I'm free and back home I'll have my work cut out for me, so I better figure out a way to get the process moving along.

There is so much to an undertaking like writing a book, I think I might be way in over my head. It takes a lot of strength and endurance to comb through the past and unearth all this shit I've accumulated. I know I have probably repeated myself, but when you're locked up like this, you can't be perfectly in tune with the surroundings. That would be just too damn comfortable for my own good. I have a little inside joke going in my head it runs like this: Do you want to hear a good one? Read "The Amazing Tragic," by Jeffrey Bovee. Perhaps that will help you remember where you've been.

It's still morning here at the jail and I just try to wait patiently for my release. It has been a hard stay here sitting in limbo. I really try to work on myself to the best of my ability, but it's tiring. I have gone through so much and I still carry a heavy burden. Everyday there's a glimmer of hope and I can feel myself healing, but it's at a snail's pace.

Last night was rough. I didn't sleep all that well and waking up to this steel and concrete can be unbearable. I find if I don't get too angry, I can usually fall back to sleep. I clear my thoughts and settle down with a prayer. I'm hoping to hear good news today about when I'll get out of here but it's a waiting game I don't like to play. The jail works on a whole different timetable. What takes a day to get outside, takes a week inside. The future ahead of me remains elusive.

I can see a short-term plan, but I never know what I'm going to get down the road. Hope and optimism are my new bedfellows and everyday clean is a healing experience that you can't put a price tag on. I'm sure no one wants to be in a jail cell, but if I don't use this time to get my head on right my thoughts will consume me, and they're not all good ones.

You have to have a thick skin inside here. There is so much that can bother you it can turn you inside out. Nobody cares about the next person and it becomes survival of the fittest. It really is sad because there is about a 90% inmate/drug addict ratio. More and more addicts are being locked up and the crimes range from stealing to murder.

I try to lift my spirit above and beyond these walls. The thought of being released is playing over and over in my head. Today is another day to be thankful I'm alive. It's a chance to discover new ways to deal with problems and cope with stress. I pray to be a vessel for love and kindness. I need help today, everyday so I can be looking forward, God willing there are many more tomorrows.

Remembering Those We've Lost

They were sons and daughters, mothers and fathers, friends and companions – people just like you and me. They died because their addiction took them out before their time. There is a list in my head, mostly junkies who are now gone and died an untimely death. Any of us could be on that list, including me. We stick needles in our arms to load our bloodstreams with substances, not knowing what our drugs are laced with poison or not.

I still get chills thinking about the last moments of life for all the people I know who have died because of heroin and opiate overdoses. You never forget the damage these drugs leave in their wake. Most of us have had some trauma or mental health issues where we used drugs to medicate an underlying problem. I guess we all felt we were better suited to treat our conditions then the health professionals. It was always a coin toss, and every time I loaded up a syringe and took a shot, I never thought that shot would take my life.

All I wanted was to feel better, to make me not feel. When drugs were coursing through my veins, I got farther and farther away from myself. I remember a nurse at Cornerstone in Rhinebeck, NY asking me, "Why do you guys hurt yourselves like this?" I had to think about that for a moment as I looked at my arms and the track marks and scar tissue on them. All I could muster up was, "I guess I don't like myself very much."

I must have endured seven detox treatments from September 2016 to March 2017. I would go in, get myself well and off the street, and return only to do it all over again. I would be high within the hour of leaving. It was a big waste of time, money, and resources. I think about it now and believe somebody could have used that treatment better than I did. It might have been the last hope for another addict or for a family who needed their kid in there. Over the years there have been at least a dozen people I know who have died from overdoses.

Four of them were this past year and the dealer continued dealing the shit out with no repercussions. I can't even tell you why I was spared after almost dying twice. I guess it just wasn't my time. I certainly am no better than those we've lost. The reason I want to write this book is to shed light on how the progression in addiction swallows up your life. Decades can come and go, and you don't even think about the time you lost till it's too late.

I'm afraid to go back out there and do the same thing all over again because I was knocking on heaven's door. When you look at death from drug addiction you will get a lot of conflicting views. There are a lot of people who will say that it serves us right for sticking needles in our arms. There are also people who feel like it's just such a waste of life. Then there are those who feel sorry for us and what we go through. Lately, I have been thinking of all the families who are scarred by this disease. The shattered dreams and the love that is lost. It's bad enough we are killing ourselves and not thinking about the people we affect as a result. Once we are taken out by this addiction it's just all too final. The sad part is we can be treated for it, but the statistics aren't very good.

Why I'm still alive today, I don't really know. God saved me and my family from a painful existence. I believe he has a use for me. Maybe I can help others? I hope it's something of that nature because I can't stand to see and read about more deaths from overdoses. It is time to try something new and completely different. I'm going to stop looking at myself as a lost addict. I can't believe I'm lesser than other people. Some of us hate what we did to ourselves, I know I do.

Remembering those we lost is a way to honor a life, a person who really did matter, but boarded the wrong train. We are not just junkies, alcoholics, and crack heads. We are real people, who at one time were little children with no idea of what was coming down the pike. Drug addiction operates in stealth. It creeps in and attaches itself to your fragile mind. You know deep in your heart and soul that something just isn't right, but you can't put your finger on it. The drugs fill the void inside you and separate you from all that is pure and sacred. It creates a false wholeness inside, and you become disoriented and lost each time you put it in your body.

You soon forget all the stories you heard about how dangerous drugs can be and roll right down into the gutter. Before you know it, people you know start dropping like flies and you can only hope you don't become one of them for a minute, maybe. The statistics out there are at epidemic proportions, but this deters no one, especially the addicts who are at the point of no return.

I had to be locked in a cage to save me from myself. I hope it doesn't have to go that way for you. I hate to admit I didn't want to live anymore before they picked me up and put me in jail. I just don't know how it could have been done differently...

2017

I spent New Year's Eve 2016 in precipitated withdrawals from Suboxone and it was an omen of worse things to come. 2016 wasn't a particularly good year for me and while I usually looked forward to a New Year, this one was different. The holidays were a bust because I was a full-blown addict and I was not properly taking my medicine prescribed by my doctor. I was a shell of my former self and all my relationships were suffering.

The holidays are supposed to be a joyous time. They are a time to enjoy family and kids. I couldn't even do that. I was selling Suboxone for heroin money and I couldn't figure out a way to stop without putting myself away. I promised my girlfriend that I would clean up and get back on track. If I didn't, I'd hit the highway.

After using heroin, I waited 24 hours like I was told, before I took Suboxone, but the next thing I knew I was in the fire of hell. Apparently, the heroin I was using was quite long acting; it had legs as we say. I should have waited longer before administering the replacement. I became violently ill and in withdrawal like I have never experienced before. I was howling, vomiting, and writhing in pain on the floor. I needed serious medical attention, but I didn't have the energy to do anything. I rode this episode out over 3-4 days into the New Year, alone in my house. My girlfriend and kids left me there and went to her folk's house because they were frightened by my condition. It was one of the most horrific things I ever put myself through.

I was really thinking I could get my shit together, but it all came crumbling down. I lasted about a week before I ran back to my dealer and picked up what I knew would work best. The destruction continued unabated. I could feel my run was coming to conclusion, though I had no idea where I would end up. I had drained every resource I had, and I was in debt like never before. I wasn't employable, but I somehow still had a job. My family was watching from the sidelines, just waiting for me to go on the disabled list.

My neighbors hated me, loathed me, call it what you will. Life was grinding to a halt, metal on metal. I had no idea how to pull myself out of the trouble I was in because I just couldn't allow the sickness to happen. I had to be straight and well in dope terminology. Each day started like the one before it with a desperate search for money, so I could get drugs in my body. I had been dragging on for so long I felt like there was no hope for me at all.

I started a series of detox visits at Cornerstone in Rhinebeck and they began to look at me like I was crazy, they saw me so much. I was there 5 times between January and March 2017. I was a complete mess and the writing was on the wall because I would not stop for anything or anybody.

March 27th was the nail in the coffin. I overdosed for the second time in six months with my children in my care. I almost died. I was arrested and thrown out of my house by CPS. It was the end of the road for me until I started to go even further into the "No Road Ahead" zone. I would soon be homeless, and I was waging a war with myself that I could never win. I landed here at the jail where I write this just for you.

Somehow, I managed to live on the streets and make things happen for my addiction. Every dime I made went right into the needle and the spoon. I barely ate. I survived on ice cream and candy bars. I communicated only with my dealers, the safe zone in heroin addiction. There is no loyalty amongst junkies. It's every addict for themselves. Self-centered and self-preservation! Camaraderie doesn't exist. When you're addicted, it's all about you.

You want what you want when you want it! It is a vicious cycle and that doesn't want to end. Looking back now, I wish I would have just listened to my girlfriend when she said she felt something bad was going to happen. I wish I would have stopped and checked into a long-term rehab. I wish I had removed myself from the streets I was running. I was a puppet, and heroin was pulling my strings. There was no self-control whatsoever.

I sold everything I owned, stole shit that wasn't mine, and put it all into that needle. I made all the half-hearted promises that every junkie makes that end with the words "tomorrow I will". I hate myself for the pain I caused but it was like being in a monster's body.

I moved to Newburgh, NY and I was running full throttle and out of control. By the time I was living with my friends on Carter Street, it was just a matter of time before somebody would be managing my life for me. I was using close to $150 a day of heroin and it was hell on earth for me. I knew I was in trouble, and then I was put to pasture. I was incarcerated two times in 2017, once in May for criminal contempt, and this most recent arrest, which brought me to this jail for petit larceny. The homelessness I experienced had me groveling in the dirt. I was into behaviors that I never had to engage in before just to survive. Living on benches, in tents, hallways, and if I was lucky a motel or shelter.

As I sit here today, in my cell, I have no outside help. I haven't spoken to my family in months. I feel abandoned, but I can't blame anyone but myself for what has transpired. The only hope I have left is God and there's no mistake that this is exactly where he wants me to be. There isn't going to be a rescue. I need to accept that. I need to deal with this accordingly and be grateful, somehow. I hope and pray daily, I give thanks that I'm still alive.

Well, it turned out that 2017 was the pivotal year where I would either sink or swim. I can give in, give up, or fight for my life. I can accept the help I need and utilize this jail cell as a way of getting healthy and learning skills I just don't have. Hopefully, I can return to my family someday down the road. I don't know how or when it will take place but that is my goal. I'm not a fortune teller and the future is always an open canvas. This life has thrown me a lot of curveballs and I've struck out every time lately.

I need to be attentive to the fact that change is inevitable. The crucial pieces of the puzzle aren't missing any more, but it will take a long time to put it together. I am an inmate but I'm grateful I'm alive and breathing. I don't want to give away the little happiness I have right now. Situations change by the minute and I don't know what to expect when I arrive in treatment. I'll be leaving this concrete jungle very soon and this is a true life-saving gift. If I pay close attention to my thoughts and sit quietly, I can look over this life and it brings a lot of different emotions. So many roads to ease my soul…

Countdown to Freedom

I just received word that I'll be leaving this jail on my girlfriend's birthday, September 19th. I'll be going to a 90-day, inpatient treatment center at St. Christopher's. I am very excited for a change in surroundings and a little taste of freedom. I'm doing my homework by asking my lawyers and offender advocates for advice to insure a smooth transition. I'm hoping there won't be any snags and that it won't be that embarrassing to arrive there in shackles.

Finally! There is some good news for a change. I wish I could share the news with my family right now, but I guess I'll have to wait till I get to the rehab. I don't have to worry about clothes or resources and that is about all I know about the place. I'm going to do everything I can to follow the rules and stay out of trouble. I know these places can be a breeding ground for negative behavior. There will be a contingency of people who are trying to save their life, and then there are the people who are escaping jails and courts.

I guess I should be thankful I'm going anywhere, because right here, right now is not the place for an addict. I try to think of the happiness inside myself spreading out like ripples in a pond to my family and friends. I also sometimes try to send telepathic messages to my girlfriend and I wonder if she hears them. All I ever really wanted was an escape hatch to real freedom. I could never direct positive energy to help myself. Many outside forces had to go to work to make this miracle happen.

My life ahead of me is a great mystery. I have lived one way and that's really all I know. I was moving so fast the years just melted away, hence the term burning the candle at both ends. All my life I've struggled to make getting high work for me. I tried it in my relationships, my daily activities, in my work, and right down to who I am. I could never keep the balance going for very long. Inevitably, the weights would shift, and I would lose balance and end up with nothing again and again.

My girlfriend would tell me that I was going to lose everything, but I couldn't and wouldn't believe any of it. Right now, I would do anything to be in Woodstock with her and the kids. To be healthy and clean. My life is a story of the good and the bad, the highs and the lows, the mountains and the valleys. I started this journey so long ago and put myself through things that would normally destroy a person.

I'm thinking of a side story I'd like to capture here - In 2009, I lived in an apartment on Yarmouth Street in Kingston, NY. I was a crack addict on opiate replacement medicine. I worked as a custodian for the local college and was making pretty good money. We decided to move, and I left a plastic bin in the garage of the property. Inside this bin, was my life's work. There was every song, poem, story, picture, trophy, news clipping and sentimental treasure I had accumulated since my childhood. The landlord went into the garage and took the bin and threw it out. I was devastated. My life's work and memories were gone. It was like having your house burn to the ground with everything you cared about in it.

It took me five years to just forgive this man for doing something I thought was unspeakable. I never entertained the thought that maybe I was getting some pay back for all the wrongs I did to people in my addiction. After this loss, I was never quite the same. I had an anger inside me that grew each year. I told myself I would just start over, but this was hard to do. I was totally wiped out emotionally from the magnitude of the loss.

It has taken me a long time to get over losing those treasures. I strongly believe this resentment accelerated my downfall. I was suffering, and I was at the mercy of an ongoing battle inside of my spirit. You can never see or tell how addiction is going to rob you. Most people claim it took everything from them. This disease, if you want to call it one, kills very decent people every day without blinking an eye.

I thank God that my life was spared, no matter how damaged and insignificant it feels. The sense of accomplishment for me was noticeable right away because I've been an addict for so long. I started feeling better the day after I let go. The most critical component of stability becomes the wind beneath your wings. I have felt angels come down to rescue me, bringing me high above the desolation so I can view it from above. With this, your spirit becomes alive and your mind opens. Your sight becomes clear. I realize it's not about getting high. I want to live.

I do think about how much time has expired and I do wish I would have seen things for what they really are. It just wasn't the right time for me. I believe God has a plan for me, and He sure the hell wasn't going to deviate from it. My path has made me the person I am today. Today is a new beginning. Rebirth does happen. Be thankful.

"May God bless and keep you always, may your wishes all come true, may we always do for others, and let others do for you.", Bob Dylan, Forever Young

A Lethal Dose

For me, addiction was a road I traveled as well as I could. It woke me up in the morning and put me to sleep at night. I regularly did things to get high that no normal person would ever do in a lifetime. I had connections in many places – I had to make sure I always had a lethal dose of alcohol and drugs available 24/7. I bought where I lived: Kingston, Port Ewen, Ulster Park, Lake Katrine, Glasco, Woodstock, Town of Ulster, Rifton, Tillson, New Paltz, Mount Marion, Lomontville, Quarryville, and Saugerties.

There was nothing and no one that was going to stop my train from rolling down the tracks. During all these pit stops, I was either in or in-between a relationship and struggling to either make it work or destroy it. I was thinking about the years of alcoholism when I drank myself into a stupor every night, just to pass out. I smoked so much marijuana during the 80s and 90s. it put me in debt every week. There were the cocaine and crack days, where I would become delirious and stay up for days on end without a shower or change of clothes. There were the heroin and prescription drugs where I would do absolutely anything to stop the sickness and withdrawals. Nothing in life mattered more than getting high when I was active.

When I consider addiction as a treatable disease, it's easier for me to look forward to a clean lifestyle. A lethal dose of heroin and fentanyl almost killed me twice within one year's time. I had been a heroin addict for 17 years at that point. All that time and I really didn't know what was in that bag of dope. These days, we're finding out that it's often not even heroin. I was taking a gamble and should have ended up in the morgue. Life doesn't have to be like that.

I'm no saint, no angel, no holy roller. I am an addict who finally surrendered. I had to be locked in this cage and forced to do it. In the coming weeks and months, I'll be going through some serious changes. I will be looking at myself in the mirror and I will relive all the things I've done, right and wrong, in this life. I will have to process events that I have no understanding of. There will be a lot of tears and triumphs. I am going to get healthy and be able to move on into the next half of this life.

I'm writing my future and it's going to be the most intense spiritual journey that will clean my house. I'm hoping that I will reunite my family and better understand myself. I will be able to let go of the guilt I have for leaving my family abandoned at so many different times. There is so much healing that still needs to take place and it's all up to me now.

The lethal doses didn't take me out, though they changed me forever. I have a lot to be thankful for and much more to live for. This life has been a rough ride with so many prayers and gear shifts, it amazes me more and more every day.

Can I Help You?

I always liked when I went to a business like a corner store, restaurant, and places like that when you're asked that simple direct question, "Can I help you?"

There have been so many times I wanted to just say, "Yes! Can you deliver me out of this horrible existence I've been living?" or "Can you please get me off alcohol and drugs?"

Sometimes, I find myself in a trance hearing those words, "Can I help you?" and I find myself looking for the deeper meaning. I remember, so many times, being in police cars, police vans, and work programs looking out the windows at all the beautiful people enjoying life without drugs. How do they do it? Am I cursed or something? You ask yourself a lot of questions when your freedom is compromised. You also make major assumptions and declarations that don't always stick. I've done time and time has definitely done me.

Getting my head on straight in the joint is no easy task. You find God damn quickly. I'm lucky I've always been a believer, it made my transition a bit easier. It still takes a leap of faith believing we can all crawl out from under the darkest days and bask in the sunshine again. This story is slowly winding down. The days are coming to an end here at the Orange County Jail. My cell #38 will be occupied by someone else and I will be on my way to long term rehabilitation. No more jail! I'm very grateful for that. Reality is, I should be doing hard time. People who knew me and my problem looked out for me.

I have no doubt in my mind they did it just as much for me as for my family, my girlfriend, and my beautiful children. I've been afforded freedoms no one may ever experience in my situation. It's these miracles you run with. You give God thanks and remember that it could be a lot worse. Addicts know it can always get worse, especially if you give it enough time. In 34 years of using drugs, you would think that I would have developed at least a little insight into how destructive it was.

I always ended up in institutions, and the next step from there is death, it's a natural fact. Some of us like to take it to the very ends of the Earth, that's me for sure. I was that type of addict; take it to the limit one more time.

I want to say I'm sorry to all the people out there who know me and read this book. Some might feel they deserve mention if I overlooked them. Some might say they shouldn't have been mentioned at all. I have a feeling I'm going to have to get a lot of releases signed. I guess we will see how that works itself out, what doesn't come out in the wash, will come out in the rinse. By no means do I wish to harm anyone, I only wish to tell my tale.

Everyone I know or dealt with usually tried to do well by me. It's me I worry about and the pain I've caused decent people. Please forgive me and know that any time spent together holds weight and gravity in music, life, laughter, love, friendship, family, and beyond. The days are numbered like the hairs on our head. Let's make use of our days and please know that I care.

I'm Almost There

Today is Thursday, September 14th, 2017. It's 8:52 AM here at the Orange County Jail in Goshen, NY and I'm sitting at my desk getting ready for another day. I'm doing my best to fortify my mind, body, and spirit for whatever comes my way. I've done this incarceration without any outside help. I'm what they call an indigent inmate, meaning you have nothing, and no one is helping you. I haven't communicated with anyone in my family for two months, neither phone nor mail.

I've reached out but there has been no reply. I think everyone has finally given up on me. It's sad but I'll survive somehow by the grace of God. It is the first time I haven't had any help while being locked up. In the past, my family were the ones who helped me through these ordeals. They kind of did the time with me, just not behind bars. When I wake up in the morning my thoughts race through my past and it all comes flooding in. It's like watching a cut up movie. I see all the crazy things I've done and can't undo.

I slow the process down and pray and it does help a bit. My story of addiction is coming to an end. It is reading more like a journal now and I feel it's long overdue. It's becoming the stream of consciousness that will hopefully carry me through the next four days until I'm at rehab. I figure I'll type it up either at the next facility or back home. I want this writing to end up in a book to help give me purpose and focus. There's a lot to be done and it needs to become priority every day for it to come to fruition. I guess we will see how it all comes together.

The drug dreams are gone. They held me captive for my first week here and now are a thing of the past. The dreams are terrifying, because I would wake up all spaced out thinking I did some. It takes on a whole different level when you have a drug dream and wake up in a jail cell.

I think about freedom and how satisfying it can be, how important it really is. You wouldn't know it from my rap sheet, but I can't stand having it taken away and giving it away so easily. The freedom to make choices alone are enough to turn most people around, it's a lot more involved with addicts, unfortunately. You don't know what you got until it's gone. Then, and only then, do you see the picture clearly, and embrace the levity of how good it is to be alive and free. I'll be there again. It won't be long.

I consider treatment to be my freedom because I'm getting my life back and I won't be in a jumpsuit and handcuffs anymore. There won't be any keys clanking, steel doors slamming, correction officers correcting, and inmates being, well, inmates... I want to remember how bad it is here, so I never repeat it ever again. The sad part about that statement is that I've said it many times before, but never followed through. This time will be different.

I have experienced a lot of loss and it will take time to rebuild again. I don't want to look ahead too far, but I know my future will unfold nicely if I put the work in and stay clean and sober. I am not going to deviate from this plan and I will recover. I went through hell to get in the headspace I'm in. I worked hand and hand with my higher power and it took a lot out of me, every incarceration takes a piece. I am an addict and there has been a monumental amount of pain and heartbreak on all fronts. I think it all needs to be aired out like dirty laundry for me to move forward. The trauma of 34 years of substance abuse, the things I've seen and done, the overdoses, and the loss of my family unit, all contribute to my suffering.

I need to look at all of this realistically and know how much weight and power they have over me. I'm powerless over my addiction I'm still feel that. I feel confident about the changes that need to be made and I never really felt like this before. The reservations are all gone. I hit the gutter at the bottom. In my youth, I was strong and could bounce back quickly and move along. I have seen so much between the ups and downs and I always kept a place in my head that my life had some meaning. I feel like I owe humanity something for taking everything from society without regard to others.

I have always been an advocate for the downtrodden and I find any cause for uplifting people interesting and inspirational. I just never jumped in with both feet and kept it moving. I became one of the addicts by default, maybe it was meant to be this way. Maybe it's easier to be uplifting by knowing what it's like.

The excitement of getting high as a kid was bad medicine. It was a secret society of learnings. I felt like I had come across the Holy Grail. My friends were all around, there was laughter and adventure, and then something changes. The drugs grow harder and stronger and it all dissipates into the biggest cloud of smoke. My soul became empty and my mind confused. It didn't take long.

I just kept pushing onward, I don't even know why really. The inevitable stories I heard became my story, and in many ways, much worse. I had to be locked down to surface my pain before I could get to the other side and reason. The insanity was woven into my life's fabric and it was suffocating me. I couldn't let go and I was on my way out of the human race. I know this now, but when you're feeding a monster it's hard to escape unscathed. The scars run deep and are only healing now as I write this.

Wisdom

If you're looking for words of wisdom you might be reading the wrong book, but the fact remains I made it out alive, again! I am one of the few, the lucky one. I was spared further pain. The police probably saved my life by locking me up. I am still here to finish my story of addiction and hopefully help someone else in the process.

We all like to think drugs are innocent and fun in the beginning. They made us feel significant in some way, like cool kids. I know it helped me to not face my feelings and problems. It put hope in the hopeless and soothed the aching heart and spirit. The trouble with drugs is they do exactly what is expected and then some. They rob your self-esteem and then promise wonderful things that are just out of your reach and you're not quite sure what they are. But you want these wonderful things, and you know more drugs will get you closer. Before you know it, you're crawling out of a gutter and spiritually destroyed.

You put all your energy and focus into keeping this illusion alive. My life is precious and worth every day above ground. I know I have a lot more to enjoy, with the good that God and this Earth have to offer. I never want to be a slave to this shit ever again; the pain is just too much.

I always considered myself intelligent and talented. Unfortunately, I was raised without an ounce of common sense. I have very poor decision-making skills and my thought process has been slightly compromised. When the chatter in your brain dies down and you're left alone to analyze and process the things you've done, you begin the slow climb out of the hell you've experienced.

You see just how far you have gone down in the food chain and you reevaluate everything about the way you live. I am a firm believer in miracles and they do appear in my lifetime all throughout my journey. The fact I can change is a miracle in itself. There is so much to enjoy and work for, it seems foolhardy too just let it all slip away.

I became very good at dulling my senses and numbing my feelings. I really don't know what else to say; the wisdom is there bubbling to the surface. I know now that if put alcohol or drugs in my body I am going to die. I'll either die from an overdose or inside an institution, with insanity trying to take my life. My writing is on my own wall - I tried to kill myself when I arrived here in my detox. There is nothing left for me to learn or gain from drug addiction.

Addiction has ruled me for more than half my life. It has taken every resource I had to keep itself alive. What kind of father would I be as a dead man, or in active addiction? I can't be with my family now, but I have a choice and chance at redemption.

Redemption! I want to get back everything I gave up for the sake of getting high. My integrity, honor, self-respect, and love were all crippled by substance abuse. I didn't give a rat's ass when I was out running the street. I just wanted the pain to stop. The bottom line is I was possessed by evil spirits. I opened Pandora's Box and a gang load of evil came churning out. Yeah man, there's a lot to be said about wisdom. I'm here to tell you there's something to be said about being beaten down and then surrendering. I'm just now coming back to life. All the gifts are intact mentally, physically, and spiritually.

Let's be honest with one another. It's the hardest decision I ever made, but the easiest way out. I'm being released from jail to a treatment facility and I can walk away at any time, get rearrested and finish out my 90 days in a jail cell to continue getting high. Most convicts here think I'm stupid to not just finish out my days in jail. They can't wait to walk out of here and do the same God damn thing and expect it not to happen again. I have been this route so many times I already know the end results.

For me, I had some sort of epiphany. God saved me and spoke in a way I could listen. Regardless of how I've changed or gained wisdom, I know what to expect if I don't get my heart and mind working in conjunction with one another. I will remember the pain I was in when I first arrived into these cells. I was beaten beyond belief with no one to pick up the pieces. People told me that this is where I was going to end up and I would not allow their thoughts in. I had to find out on my own again and again.

I experienced so much pain by not listening, it's not even funny. In the first week of incarceration here I was making deals with the devil – "Let me out and I promise I will change," kind of stuff.

Somehow God interceded and said this one is mine take. He taught me the basic survival skills and I started to believe and change. It didn't hurt that I was aware of being an addict of 34 years either, those numbers alone were scary. You can't do drugs for that long and expect to be the picture of health in 30 days. I need to grow into my new self if that's what it takes to be totally free again. I'm probably not even half way there yet, but I don't worry because getting through a day at a time is enough for me.

I noticed my eyes clear up first, the windows to the soul. I look into the mirror and say, "I'm worth it today." I don't have to beg for God to take me anymore, because I'm following His master plan. This is the kind of wisdom I have acquired. This is a life-saving experience that can keep me free forever. I remember all too much the days of despair and derangement. I hope I covered enough of it in this story.

I know I could have just focused on the "dirt" and that would satisfy a lot of people. I certainly did entertain that, but I couldn't just focus on the war stories. I figure there's a healthy heap of them for the population's appetite. I think there are enough meat and potatoes inside this tale to fill them up. It really came down to if it would help or hamper me. This story has been like a fourth step in Narcotics Anonymous - a searching and fearless moral inventory.

The only difference being it's for everyone to see. It has me wondering if it's necessary, but I plow on with good intentions. This has revealed all the dark caverns of what it took for me to survive as an addict. There are the cons, the burns, the manipulations, the false promises, and, well, you get the picture. When these demons get exposed to the light, they disintegrate.

I think this tale will be a bit much for your average reader but addiction touches so many families these days I hope it won't be frowned upon. Today I am a ward of the court, the county of Orange, in the state of NY. It's unsettling. I'm praying I will get the best care possible. The sheriff is going to transport me to St. Christopher's in Putnam County, Garrison NY and I'm told I'll be arriving in shackles so that should be an interesting day! I have been accepted and the date is set for me to start treatment on September 19th, 2017, Stephanie's birthday.

Hopefully, it will all go down without a hitch, stranger things have happened to me. I have court in two jurisdictions, The Town of Newburgh and Family Court in Ulster County. The outcomes of both ride on my participation in treatment and getting well. I'm praying I can reunite with my family. I have to believe in things working out for various reasons and the lessons of wisdom continue all day, 24/7, 365 days a year. I got to believe.

Living with Bad Choices

Yes, sir! I knew this one was coming down the road! The hundreds of (mostly bad) choices you make as an addict becomes a constantly growing mass of baggage. Even the suitcase seems to rip and tear, trying to spill out the past, but I keep everything stuffed inside, out of everyone's view. The forgiveness it takes to shed this baggage is monumental, mountainous – I don't think there is a word invented that properly describes this. But it's the only way to heal, to forgive one's self and others for the poor decisions made in the past.

I was looking back in all directions and I'm not going to trim the fat - bad choices were my best friend. I used them to clarify and justify my position in the game. I made and used them to solidify and advance myself in the game. It was all a game. These choices I've made have affected everyone I've touched. I must accept responsibility for my choices and actions today. If I don't the healing won't even begin to take place.

Bad choices were my best friend. I made and used them to justify myself in my game. Every choice I made affected someone, either directly or indirectly and I need to accept the responsibility that comes with making these choices. If I just look the other way, I'll never heal. Come to find out, the hundreds (thousands!) of bad choices I've made have turned into a midnight train carrying a shitload of baggage. It's time to pull into the station and unload.

Of the many choices I've made along this path, a few standout as true turning points. Looking back, it should have been so easy to take the clean road. The first bad choice was in succumbing to peer pressure with friends and family. This flipped a switch in me that got stuck in the "ON" position for decades. This first choice was probably the biggest as well. Once I got started, I didn't want to quit.

My next mistake was in continuing down the path of addiction without asking for help. I didn't know how addiction was going to damage me. My girlfriend and sons weren't in my life at that point. I was just a kid and my brain cells weren't even fully developed, so I didn't know this was a question to ask. But I should have recognized this was not the right way. At the time, it seemed ok.

There is no way to make it out of a situation like that when you're innocently involved. I was predetermined to be the companion for the journey. I wouldn't wish this on anyone, but my recovery depends on me accepting this path that I chose.

Next, I chose to separate myself from society and I was ok with this. I didn't like what I saw in the mainstream and found a band of brothers that shared my like of drugs. There are many people who helped me to disassociate myself from what I saw as "square." I neglected my own feelings and now I feel like a man with the brain of a child.

I wish my parents had helped me better recognize these critical choices earlier. My dad tried to turn me around, but he worked too much to supervise and discipline. My mother had no issues with alcohol and marijuana use, even for us kids. I know they did what they could, but they really weren't ready to raise kids. They were both hard-working people that were just escaping from their own childhoods. And I was left to make my own decisions with limited guidance. I had to figure out the shit parts of life through my own experience.

I got launched into adulthood at 16 and I was far from capable of making the informed choices a teenager would make in a solid household. I look back and see that relationships were the breeding grounds for my poor choices about half the time. I never felt good about myself and I had trouble communicating how I felt. I was shy and introverted. My relationships started as alcohol and drug-fueled romps. I never could understand the mechanics of life's lessons when I was young. I could tell you stuff was "far out" or "cool man", but my growth was stunted because of ingesting drugs so early on.

As I grew, my bad choices moved grew in the way I impacted others. I began stealing things, although mostly just small stuff and it became a normal behavior to me. This came with the territory as money felt like it was just leaking out of my pockets. These early crimes involved my family because I knew the consequences wouldn't involve criminal justice systems. It was a convenient sandbox to play in.

While I've been writing this book, I've often wished I was just another reader of the storyline. This effort has taken a lot out of me and forced me to look back and remember the most painful and harrowing of times. I try to put the spin on it and tell myself it's all necessary to begin the process of healing and change. Bad choices follow you and stick to you like the plague. You can't underestimate the gravity drugs hold in your life.

The general story is that Jeffrey Bovee is a good guy when he's not high on alcohol/drugs. But when he is, he's a piece of shit. I got used to the stories over the years; the negative talk was already in my own head so hearing it elsewhere just solidified the fact. I really didn't care the bad choices were like a second set of skin. It hurts to write that and acknowledge the truth it held. There was no one left in the end. No one wanted to be around me, and I didn't want to be around them much, either. It is because of this I know why no one communicates with me while I'm institutionalized.

Most friends and family believe the real Jeffrey Bovee is gone forever. The good guy never had a chance; he's no longer with us. Well, I want to assure every single one of you non-believers that I'm alive and well and it's all about self-preservation today! My renewal and a new me is here to stay. I have a fighting chance at recovery and restoration!

As I learn from my mistakes and forgive myself, my bad choices will not stalk me like prey anymore. If I can see them for what they were and how they were decided upon, I can take responsibility, quietly ask for forgiveness and move on knowing I will not fall into that trap again.

Life is strange and mysterious. I have to attain a level of hope and faith sufficient to rebuild from the ruins. I must keep instilling this faith into my brain to remind myself that I can do this recovery thing. I have come a long way from 1983 and went through so many changes it blows my mind still. I recognize this jail cell has opened doors for me that were once closed. The freedom box has been cruel and kind at the same time.

I know this because I'm inmate 2017-03954 C2-Cell 38 Orange County Jail. Every night I thank the Lord for getting me through another day and night. I wake up and my intentions and focus are on what changes I have to make today so I can have a tomorrow. In the future, maybe I will be able to help others. Stranger things have happened…

The Kids are Alright

My two kids are back home in beautiful Woodstock, NY. They are probably just getting up and ready for their day at school. I used to love being awake and ready to help them prepare for the day in the early morning. They are my world, even today behind bars, even though most people think I've failed them. I can't envision a life without them, but here I am seven months later and I'm not even close to returning or having a normal life with them.

I'm going to need to find my way through family court because they need to insure there will be no more neglect and that I'm safe to be around. The courts will have no sympathy. They know what happens next. Here's a guy who overdosed with his children in his care and traumatized them forever. I burn inside knowing how much I have hurt them.

They didn't deserve to witness my bad choices and somehow down inside me, I know they could tell their Dad was "different" at times. My oldest son was well-aware I had a problem and was doing something I shouldn't have been involved with. It still causes me to have a lot of guilt and shame. It's hard to accept the circumstances and the fallout from them.

I force myself to learn from what took place. I have to grow into a new pair of shoes again. I'm hoping my kids turn out alright and are resilient enough to get through the days without me.

Back then, I was moving and using at such a clip I couldn't tell if I was coming or going. I was always plotting my next move - where the money was coming from and how I was going to sleep and wake up well.

It's a dirty business that made me a full-time worker that had my full attention. I try to think about what heroin and opiates taught me.

It sure the hell showed me a dirty way to live and dulled the feelings I was trying to avoid. I ask myself what pain I was trying to avoid. On the outside, I had the perfect life, but the inside was never paid much attention to. The feelings of being a failure and never living up to my potential were broad in scope and always digging at me. I never set goals and I lost faith in my journey.

My life was always coming to a boil, but it took a long time before it came to a head. I always wanted to be clean and sober. I would take a shot at cleaning up and tell myself "Look at your family. This is the center of your universe." But I would hear myself reply, "Is this all that's left for you?" I couldn't see up from down, good from bad, or life from death. It was all about getting the next high.

And, all the while, I'm thinking about my girlfriend and children, and how I left them to fend for themselves. Even worse, I've become a burden. I've missed amazing opportunities just for the sake of getting out of my head. But, today, I've been afforded a chance to get my life in order and I'm running with it.

What's it going to take to get my family unit back together? Whatever it is, it is imperative. I'll have to work as hard at recovery as I did my addiction, without the immediate reward and rush. I haven't been killed in this fight, but I took some really hard shots.

If I'm completely honest, I was a volunteer in my story, not a victim. I put the needle in my arm and let it take everything I loved. I know it was wrong, and it bothers me at a deep gut level. I still am amazed at the gravitational pull of drugs. They are so strong and seductive. Then they betray you and turn your soul inside out. Are the kids alright? I sure the hell hope so, I hope they can hold on.

Reality Check

I wanted to write a chapter called "Reality Check" for no other reason than to avoid the chapter name "The Real Dirt". I have tried to stay away from "war stories' in graphic detail because it's just too grisly. Last night, I had a dream about shooting cocaine. I haven't had a drug dream in weeks.

There are two things I haven't mentioned yet. Both took place in 2017. I shot cocaine for the first time and I smoked angel dust. Two more things to add to the list of things I said I'd never do. Well, I did, and I probably would have done them more if the opportunity existed. I am a garbage head at heart; my drugs of choice follow a progression from decade to decade. Let's see how they look in chronological order to get a better understanding.

1983-1993 Alcohol/marijuana/psychedelics

1993-2003 Alcohol/marijuana/cocaine

2003-2013 Cocaine/prescription
opiates/heroin/methadone maintenance/Suboxone

2013-2017 Heroin/prescription opiates/Suboxone/cocaine

This is the visible progression as it took place in my life over the last 34 years. It blows my mind to see the progression and the changes in substances. You can really see how the hard drugs eventually win over everything.

When I was an active alcoholic, I often thought about what it would be like to be a heroin addict. I knew it gave you the body high I always tried to attain through drinking. I used to drink so much I would get a feeling of weightlessness and be unable to move a muscle before I'd pass out. I would wake up every morning still in my clothes from the previous night. I would wake up in strange environments and flee into the morning, hung-over and broke.

For a long time, alcohol provided all the relief I needed. I became good at drinking and it allowed me to get over some insecurities I had socially. There are so many instances of poor decision making in my story it probably should have been called "The Poor Decisions of Jeff Bovee". I couldn't for the life of me see things for what they truly were. My vision and comprehension were so far gone I was operating more like a machine than a human being. In this state, you can't see beyond the tragedies happening weekly and you pretend you're ok when you're around loved ones and friends.

I know everyone could see it bursting at the seams, they just didn't know what to do. The nature of addiction is to bring the addict to a conclusion. But our closing scenario ends up waiting to see how long it take for the devastation to shut you down. I know for me I was losing and rebuilding over and over. I would then proceed to knock it all down again. The half-hearted attempts at cleaning up afforded me nothing but to waste more time. These attempts never last or stick, when you need the drug in your system you will go to any length to get it.

When you need a fix, all material possessions and everything that's sacred to you mean nothing. We would sell the shirt off our backs when were dope sick. It's a fact, junkies go crazy when the dope runs out and they worry about tomorrow. The extreme nature of the beast is beyond scary when you're in the throes of it. The crimes that are committed in desperation when there is nowhere to go or turn set up the solution for treatment. If you're lucky you get locked up and forced to clean up.

The alternatives are sketchy when you're running the streets homeless and addicted. I don't like to talk about this as a reality, because I found out long ago the truth hurts. I want so bad to be out of this cell I'm in and feel the grass under my feet. I must accept that everything is on God's timetable and I can't will myself out of this situation. I can get stronger mentally, physically, and spiritually but I can't escape literally.

To be truthful, I didn't think I would be locked down this long for such a petty crime. The reality is the judge knew I was strung out and stole for drugs and wanted me to clean up. These judges see this stuff all the time. It's written all over your being when you step in front of him. Let it be a lesson to you, I wouldn't want anyone to have the experiences I went through. I hope it's a wakeup call for my fellow addicts out there. There is an easier and softer way, it's called rehab. Try it, it might be the best time you put in anywhere. Reality and truth can be a bitch, but it can also save your life.

Didn't Want You to Leave

In life, and especially the life of an addict, there are recurring themes that fuel the constant ebb and flow of self-deconstruction. There are deep rooted feelings of abandonment, loss, fear, pain, love, anger, and an assortment of other emotions. I know that as a child I felt very alone for some reason. There were always people walking in and out of my life from an early age. It happens when you move a lot, you put roots down somewhere, they flourish and grow, and then Bam! They are ripped out of a perfectly fertile ground.

Sometimes you just don't have any control over things because you're a kid and at the mercy of your caregivers and family. You can only hope they bestow upon you a level of love and caring that generates security. "Didn't Want You to Leave" is a song I wrote in 1999 when I first really started to get into opiates. It was written as a reminder to me about the women in my life up until that point.

The song was written to touch on the abandonment and insecurity that I felt. It came out so naturally, not forced at all, powerful and deep, a song of hope and repair. When you're an addict, you feel almost less than everyone else, it makes you feel different than the rest of the world, the general community you keep at large.

I stare out of these hollow eyes searching for some kind of truth that continues to evade me. How am I going to fill the void that drugs did for me?? It feels unnatural and unnerving to be clean in the early stages. I have spent hours and days with my wife going over the age-old question "What propels me as an addict?" It's not as simple as the drugs. There is a deeper hidden answer and I find it even hard today to figure out.

133

I find it hard to give a straight answer because I'm just not in touch with my feelings enough to answer. Sometimes, I feel like I was born this way because it's gone on for so long. I don't like touching on insecurity and deeper heartfelt shit that I've endured. All my relationships with people were touched by my use and abuse in one way or another. I count down the years and I see how damaged a unit I am.

I do believe nothing is beyond repair and usually most of us addicts have something to offer in this world. We were someone else before we put the drugs in our systems. We can find a way to love, heal, and live again. There is help, we just have a problem asking for it most of the time. I am still alive after 34 years of "the high cost of low living."

Right now, as I write this, I'm gearing up for my 47th birthday. It's going to be a clean one because I will be in treatment. Nonetheless, it will be something to celebrate and be proud of. It's extremely hard to remember any clean birthdays in my past except for the ones I was locked up for. It is pretty frightening to think that more than three quarters of my life I've lived as an addict not knowing truly who I am. It is a reality I had to come to grips with and I have to do it daily.

How did so much time slip while I wasn't minding the store? How much wasted time? If I wasn't a writer, musician, father, and son how much of my life would really count? If I wasn't a creative person how much have I contributed to society? I have so many questions and so few answers.

Today, I wrote another letter to my mother trying to communicate to her that I'm sorry for everything I've put her and my family through. I've sent dozens of these same letters during incarcerations, and institutional stays. She could just read an old one with the same message... Whatever the outcome may be, at the very least I reached out to her and tried to let her know that I care. She will always be Mom and she's the last parent alive in my family.

I don't want to waste another day fighting this disease. I have to surrender completely. I prepare myself for the inevitable probability that I have lost my loved one's support because of my choices. I'm not even sure if my girlfriend and children will be available to me when I finally make it back to the area I lived. I love them all so much, but I was not stable, and I was neglectful in my duties as a parent. My girlfriend never had the depth of the problems I've had because she was never an addict. Sure, we partied a bit here and there, but she could turn the switch off and I couldn't. In hindsight, she never looked like she enjoyed it very much either.

I have to say I'm happy about that because my children are with a responsible and clean parent. They are well taken care of and I know down inside they miss me and want me back home with them. The greatest thing I can do for my children and my family is stay clean and get healthy and strong. I have gone through hell and back to get this small amount of serenity that I'm experiencing, even in a jail cell!

My writing has opened the floodgates of feelings and experiences. It has been therapeutic, and I can't put a price tag on this kind of freedom. Every day I write I'm free. I leave this small cell and the negativity behind for the length I can keep the pen rolling. I write my story to convey a message to others that they might think twice about addiction in general.

It hasn't been easy pouring out my heart and soul; it takes a lot out of me on many different levels. The thing is, it helps to relive some of this shit, so I can make peace with myself. It also passes time I otherwise would just be swimming in my head and depressed about my current situation. Once I fix myself, I want to help next eleven-year-old kid avoid addiction.

I wrote so much today my head and hand hurts. I wrote this book by hand as a lefty and it's sore to say the least. There are no type writers here on this cellblock! No stinking dictation help, cell phones, or hand-

Jeffrey Bovee

held recording equipment. I laid it out like my pen was dipped in my own blood. I want to thank God for helping me to keep it real.

Songwriting: Are Drugs Good for Creative People?

My favorite album of all time is probably "Exile on Main Street," by the Rolling Stones. It was released in 1971 and is an album fueled by alcohol, cocaine, and heroin. It was recorded in the basement of a mansion on the French Riviera. This album is filled with drug references and you can feel it in the grooves of the vinyl when you listen. It's a masterpiece in the rock n roll canon.

At the time, Keith Richards and other members of the band were recording this in an opiate haze. The album was made on Keith's time and it was a communal living environment. I bring this up to address the title of this chapter and to dig deeper into the issue of drugs and creative endeavors. There have been hundreds of musicians and writers who have been touched in one way or another by drug addiction.

A lot of us have said it was a creative tool before it took things to a different level. The fact is, drug use can lubricate creativity in the early stages. Hell, some of our best work has been when we discovered that opiates seemed to open a flood of ideas. I myself have written two albums worth of songs in a year's time under the influence of heroin. The problem is it comes with a price. Nothing is free or gainful once the addiction sinks its claws into you.

Some of our heroes in the literary and music community have been ravished by substance abuse in one form or another. Some people feel that people with weak constitutions or the lack of willpower are the most affected. I'm here to tell you differently and to destroy the myth. This disease is something that becomes so deep, it's in your DNA. You're being invaded by a drug genome of sorts. I believe some of us were predestined to become addicts, it happens very naturally, unfortunately. The shit has been around since the dawn of time. It's passed down from generation to generation. People like to feel good; drugs do that for a short period of time.

Eventually, we all succumb to the pain and pleasure dance, the principal and law of the drug hierarchy. The drugs we use are illegal unless their prescribed. Most of the ways and wants to get them are illegal also. The most beautiful and coolest thing is when you hear that an actor, musician, or writer comes out clean for good on the other side.

They are great minds and talented people who suffered for years at the hands of this disease and were able to beat it. They still are creative and some of them have done their best work as a result. I know I have argued and many others that once they stopped getting high their art went down the toilet. They say they lost their edge and it's just not the same. Listen man, sobriety isn't for everyone, but its' pretty hard to be creative when you're stealing to get high and living on a park bench freezing from the cold.

I struggle from the inside thinking about what my life will look like now that I'm stripped of my addiction, my best friend. I am a firm believer that life will and can get better by what I've seen. The most destitute junkies and alcoholics become successful, happy, and honorable pillars in society. That is what I want, the chance to achieve that kind of greatness and peace of mind. A chance to be of service to mankind at large, it's the only way out for me.

Creatively, I wouldn't have been able to write my story if I was still out there getting high. I wouldn't find the time in-between looking, searching, and using the drugs 24/7. You quickly learn when you're an addict that there's things you can and can't do. Writing songs and performing at clubs and bars was a huge part of my life and I did it all on drugs. For some reason it went hand and hand, probably because it started from the very beginning.

I can't over emphasize the direct correlation of the two. In the beginning it was all about alcohol and marijuana, greasing the chain so to speak, the definitive gateway of my youth. I started writing well before I started using, but when the switch was turned on, I went to town! It was a flood of pictures, ideas, and adventures, the visionary place I always attained for.

I was filling up notebooks faster than I could find one, page after page of songs, stories, and observations. It all felt completely natural and not forced in the least. Everything was so new and exciting, it felt like I was coming of age and I was only a teenager when the wheel started to really spin.

But recently, I needed drugs just to get me feeling well enough to even practice playing. I've only written a handful of songs in the past seven years. If I didn't have my shit together, everything was on hold until I got high again. People I played with were well-aware I was always about to fall out, like I always did, time after time.

I'm a talented and productive musician. I play keyboards, guitar, and I'm a singer/songwriter. I've been at it since I was sixteen years old. Music and writing are my life's work, my calling, my one love that has never turned its back on me. Music has brought a considerable amount of joy and freedom into my life. The drugs were an allure - something that everyone needed for idea lubrication. In the end, drugs were the only thing that kept the ball rolling and I was lost without them.

When you're an addict, everything else stands in line and waits for that next fix or hit. There is nothing more important than that shit coursing through your veins. It's your life's blood, your survival piece. I find it to be a real drag that I put that kind of emphasis on my drug use instead of getting the real help I needed from the jump. I can't change anything now I have to write and live by a new narrative.

The tsunami that was me destroyed everything in its path, the reconstruction has begun. I have to pick up all the broken pieces and put it all back together somehow, someway. I put my faith in my higher power and asked him to feed and nurture me back to health. I was given a gift that no longer can be squandered. Today, more than ever I want to be me again. I have a whole readjustment period to go through. I've been far away in outer space riding the cosmos. It's time to come back and plant my feet firmly on the ground.

It is going to be a process, creativity at its finest. When asked the rhetorical question "Do drugs help creativity," the answer is yes and no. I can only speak for myself and from experience. I think most addict/musicians would agree that until the drugs overtook our lives and it became a full-time job to keep up with it was a vital, viable, and useful tool. The payoff of continuing our work clean and sober affords us a much larger gift and you can remember what it was that moment and beyond.

Being clean offers a degree of freedom that is without boundaries. Being a creative person doesn't have to come with a curse or malady. You are free to test the waters with the spirits and elixirs that are out there but take it from me, it's a bummer down the road apiece. When you're a junkie kicking in a jail cell begging God for mercy, remember it's not a joke. This is a reality you don't want to step foot into. I am telling you firsthand please don't test these waters!

Last Words and Thoughts

This book has opened so many memories and moments in my life that were touched by drugs and the addiction thereafter. I received a glimpse of how much prayer and meditation has afforded me to get to this point of the story. Once you make the decision to turn your will over and surrender to your higher power, the whole game changes.

The 34 years I spent getting high took up the better part of my life and as a result I have a lot of experience on the using end and barely at all in recovery. I have to start somewhere, and this was the way to do it. I was beaten down and I lost the fight. The disease kicked my ass. I came into this jail cell broken and begging for mercy. I was in in severe withdrawal. In admitted powerlessness, I looked towards a new beginning.

I had to find hope amidst the ironic gift of desperation. I had to go through hell and back to force surrender. I certainly found no other way to be more effective. I got stronger and more vigilant in wanting to heal. I remembered the pain of the streets and how hard it really was to look inside myself for an answer.

The days of worrying about my next fix are in the past, I do it one day at a time now. It wasn't so long ago for me when I sat on the toilet in a filthy bathroom trying to find a good vein to inject and saying to myself "Is this all that's left for me?"

My incarceration forced me to get the ball rolling along. The only other way was to end up dead. I had been everywhere else, and I couldn't help myself or get into treatment the regular way. My life had become meaningless and my soul was lost. My family wanted nothing to do with me because of all the damage I brought to their lives. I asked God to help me in all these things.

I came to believe that maybe all this recovery stuff wasn't bullshit after all. Miraculously, He did for me what I couldn't do for myself. He saved me from certain death and lifted me up out of active addiction. As I gear up for one more day in jail, I would like to touch on some things I might have overlooked.

There have been so many situations, events, people, places, and things that have garnered so much weight and domination in my mind it wouldn't be right to not allow them to surface. I have lived in many geographic locations and I have come to know a lot of people through my work and my music. I have had friends, family, and neighbors watch over and help me and my family it's difficult for me to sort it all out.

These people watched from the sidelines as I destroyed everything in my path. They have never looked down on me or even questioned me because they figured it would all end up exactly as it has. I would be doing hard time in state prison if God and decent people didn't bail me out. I was the type of addict that would pray for the pain to end each day. I had a real hard run at the end and I promised God I would seek help.

I often asked for him to take my life also because I couldn't bear to live another day addicted. Addiction robbed me of everything. Over and over, again. And, I was a participant eager to give it all away. In my addiction I was a liability and a burden in my relationships and society at large. It has been extremely difficult and sad to look back over all these years and view the destruction. I tried to be as honest and thorough as possible.

I've left out my employers in this story because of their business and status. I don't want to call out names and end up on the end of litigation or cause more harm than I already have. In the last three years, I caused nothing but problems for anyone I worked for. My employers were saints and I have nothing but respect for them. I owe a deep debt of gratitude and I hope they will forgive me when I finally get around to making amends to them.

The things you endure to keep a train like me moving are unfathomable. My train crossed the country and dumped me head first into the repair station twisted and crushed. When you clean up, do your best to look objectively at all areas of your existence. The manipulations, thefts, dishonesty, and delirium are uncovered and exposed in the light.

The reclamation of the soul is the hardest work I've ever done. Since the time I started using drugs until I was brought to this jail cell, I have been involved with some grimy shit all in the name of staying selfishly high as a kite. It is sad to hear the refrains of "No one takes your word seriously," or "No one will leave you alone in their house," or "No one will lend you even a Dollar." It is a fact of life that I hate but have to accept.

Today I can be proud that I'm clean and I want to live a different life. I want people to know Jeffrey Bovee as someone who climbed out of the gutter and turned his life around. I will and can get better, stronger, respectful, trustworthy, healthy, and helpful. I want to reinvent myself because the person I know is much different than the image others know.

I came through people's lives like a tornado. I turned everything upside down and inside out. The center of a distorted and collapsing universe, I came to cataclysmic end. I had to be locked up and believe there was a good reason behind it. I feel like getting another chance is exactly what was needed at just the right time.

I've had enough down, and I will remember where I came from even if it kills me. I know the real work begins at rehab and after I'm back on the streets. Every day, I have to keep my pain up front and in view to remind myself how really bad it was. Somehow the size my of consequences is now supremely different – more enormous than ever

Jeffrey Bovee

before. I could be dead, game over, incommunicado, and the curtain goes down on this scene. This reality is all too familiar amongst us addicts.

I hope my last words and thoughts convey the grim message of continuing as I did with the hope that there really is a better life available to us also in recovery. It makes no difference if I'm writing this from a jail cell or in a rehab really. The fact is the timing was right, the words came to me and I had to figure this out with a degree of pain and separation. To all my friends, family, band members, associates, past employers, and whoever else will listen I love you all and I hope you are pulling for me like I do for you. God bless and stay on the sunny side of the street.

The Amazing Tragic

Onto the same broken lands,
Where we laugh again,
The sea is blue and green,
The thoughts are in-between.
I thought I seen your face,
But in the wrong place,
I couldn't talk or free myself,
There was nowhere safe

- J. Bovee from "Amazing Tragic," 1999

These haunted words are from my song, "The Amazing Tragic." This song appears on my first album, "One Lost Summer" that was released in 2001. I always loved this title and the song applies to my story well.

It is finally looking like this journey in writing is over! The story of Jeffrey Bovee, born October 4th, 1970 follows an uneven timeline of use and abuse for the better part of 34 years. Writing these pages was probably the most difficult and most rewarding experience of my life. It gestated in prison and came out in daily spurts.

I'm really hoping and counting on reaching as many people as possible. I want to help people like me who are addicts and people whose lives were touched by addiction in one way or another. It's a story of the loss of innocence, despair, destruction, reconstruction, hope, and faith. It is a journey through the darkest night to the rising of the sun and a brand-new day.

I tried my hardest in writing this to be as clear and concise and unapologetic as humanly possible. We all know the "I'm sorry" bit more times than we would like to count. My hopes were to carry a message of reconciliation to the lives I touched and my own spirit. I was able to get through the process with faith and acceptance to my surroundings.

I have been a writer for a long time and it coincided with my exposure to drugs and alcohol as well. It took a huge leap of faith to get this all written down on paper. I worked feverishly from the middle of August 2017 through the 18th of September. I wrote 3-4 times a day, hours upon hours. This is my first real experience writing a book, so I'm absolutely certain there is a fair amount of ground that was retreaded and over analyzed. But I hope it captures my process.

This wasn't an easy task. In the beginning it was hard to motivate myself, it felt very overwhelming. I prayed for help and guidance and tried very hard to get as much out without staying to long on specifics. I guess I'm trying to say that it wasn't a very descriptive piece of literature. I know it's far from a masterpiece, but we live in an imperfect world. I would like to think there's a message of hope somewhere in here being it was written entirely in a jail cell and minimally edited to retain the gut and core of what I felt at the time.

I still haven't read it cover to cover to see what I think about it. I'm guessing by the time it hits an editor's table and I'm fishing for a publisher that some door will open, and it will be something to be proud of. It doesn't bother me to think there is much more work to be done, I anticipated it. These sorts of undertakings are new to me. I am a writer for sure, but I have spent nearly my entire life as a singer/songwriter/performer.

I patterned this book after two of my favorites. They bounced around yet stayed simple and direct. Everything has a beginning and ending in this life. I know my story is far from over, but I didn't want this one to stretch past my final day incarcerated. I am in territories I know little about, and I am not the same as I was when I started it. I am about to go through even more changes as I transition into a rehab.

I know there's a lot of joy and more pain to come. I am not immune to the suffering just because I'm not sticking needles in my arm anymore. I don't know where the spinning wheel stops. Life is a mystery, a gamble, an unanswered letter, and a dreamer's dream. We are all in it together and the road goes on forever.

The Beginning

It's 5:30 AM, September 18, 2017 here at the Orange County Jail in Goshen, NY and I can't sleep another wink, so I decided to proceed with the last of my writing or the afterword as some call it.

First, I want to say it has been an honor and privilege to communicate my story onto these pages. When I first arrived here, I was broken and desperate, a shell of the man I should be. When I decided to start writing it freed me from the concrete and steel, the razor wire and the endless clanking keys and radio chatter. While I was scribbling away, I could detach myself from my surroundings and feel like I wasn't incarcerated. Half the battle was getting out of the prison I set up in my own head.

I'm leaving tomorrow for 90 days of rehab and I will be afforded a freedom I can only wish for in these remaining hours. Usually, I can just lie here on my steel bed and sleep until the intercom wakes me up for breakfast. Today, I have too much energy flowing through me. I told myself I was going to read this whole story before I leave, but I think I'll wait until I get it typed up and in a better format. It's all chicken scratch on loose leaf paper and pads.

Being an addict has taught me a lot of very painful and deep lessons. I search for answers to all these tormented questions, how, when, where, and why did it all go wrong and change from an innocent enough start. In the end it was like feeding a monster inside me. I fed it just to feel like normal otherwise it turned me inside out. I don't know why it chose me or I chose it, but it's been a part of me so long I didn't know any other way to live.

Jeffrey Bovee

I was afraid of the changes and the unknown prospects that come with putting the drugs down once and for all. I've visited so many jails and institutions that I started to think I would never make it to the point I'm at today. It really was like waiting for a miracle to happen and I feel like it finally did.

In closing and finally making it to the end of something, I want to say I love you. All of us who have been struggling so hard and have put our addiction before everything else. I'm pulling for you over here behind the walls. There is no greater liberty and feeling than freedom. If you are a prisoner in your own mind and body or running amok on the streets, you know what I'm talking about. I want to remind everyone to wake up to God and thank him for sparing you further pain and suffering.

To those no longer with us, I want to glorify your life and wish you peace in eternal life. The days turn into months and the months turn into years very quickly, so don't blink. Everything happens when you're not minding the store and the next thing you know the shelves are empty. I look in the mirror and see the heavy lines and the gray stubble on my chin and the missing teeth. I never imagined I would be here in a jail cell writing my life story.

Please, my friends, tread lightly, seek wisdom and peace, and above all love like your very life depends on it. Stay strong and stay clean. God bless you and keep you always.

J.B. 9/18/2017

Made in the USA
Middletown, DE
30 January 2019